American Lives 1

Readings and Language Activities

Gail Feinstein Forman
Developmental Reading and English Language Instructor
San Diego City College

New Readers Press

This book is based on a concept and outline created by Gail Feinstein Forman.

New Readers Press has used all reasonable skill and care to ensure that the historical information presented in this book is accurate. A list of the references consulted and the notes identifying the sources of quotations appears on pages 109–112.

Cover Topical Press Agency/Stringer/Hulton Archive/Getty Images; pp. 4, 11, 18, 32, 39, 46, 53, 67 © 2005 www.clipart.com; p. 4 Courtesy of Massachusetts Historical Society; p. 11 Library of Congress, Prints & Photographs Division, Detroit Publishing Company Collection, LC-D416-29459; p. 18 Library of Congress, Prints and Photographs Division LC-USZ62-7407; p. 25 Courtesy of Springfield Library; p. 25 Library of Congress, Prints and Photographs Division LC-USZ62-78299; p. 39 Library of Congress, Prints and Photographs Division LC-USZ62-119343; p. 46 Library of Congress, Prints & Photographs Division, Detroit Publishing Company Collection, LC-D414-K3490; p. 53 Library of Congress, Prints and Photographs Division, LC-DIG-ggbain-00701; p. 60 Library of Congress, Prints & Photographs Division, NYWT&S Collection, LC-USZ62-120837; p. 60 Topical Press Agency/Hulton Archive/Getty Images; p. 67 Legends Archive; p. 74 American Philosophical Society; p. 74 Library of Congress, Prints & Photographs Division, Edward S. Curtis Collection, LC-USZ62-49042; p. 81 Library of Congress, Prints & Photographs Division, NYWT&S Collection, LC-USZ62-127236; p. 81 Library of Congress, Prints & Photographs Division, NYWT&S Collection, LC-USZ62-127237; p. 88 NASA; p. 95 © 2005 JupiterImages Corporation, a wholly-owned subsidiary of Jupitermedia Corporation; p. 95 Taken by Robert Foothorap; p. 102 A. Dennis Gaxiola

American Lives: Readings and Language Activities, Book 1
ISBN 978-1-56420-435-6

Copyright © 2005 New Readers Press
New Readers Press
ProLiteracy's Publishing Division
104 Marcellus Street, Syracuse, New York 13204
www.newreaderspress.com

Printed in the United States of America
9 8

Proceeds from the sale of New Readers Press materials support professional development, training, and technical assistance programs of ProLiteracy that benefit local literacy programs in the U.S. and around the globe.

Writer: S. Dean Wooton
Acquisitions Editor: Paula L. Schlusberg
Content Editor: Beth Oddy
Design and Production Manager: Andrea Woodbury
Photo Illustrations: Brian Quoss
Illustrations: Carolyn Boehmer, Amy Simons
Production Specialist: Brian Quoss, Jeffrey R. Smith
Cover Design: Kimbrly Koennecke

Contents

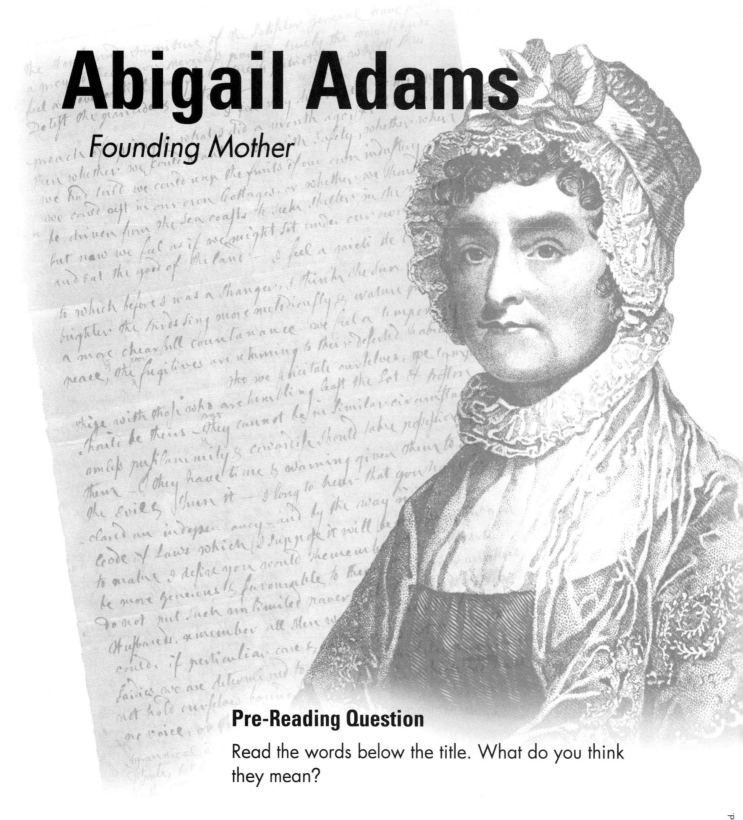

Abigail Adams
Founding Mother

Pre-Reading Question

Read the words below the title. What do you think
they mean?

Reading Preview

Abigail Adams lived during difficult times. She married a
leader who helped form the United States. She watched
these events happen. And she wrote letters that tell us
about the people and events of the time.

Abigail Adams

Abigail Adams saw the birth of the United States. Her letters help us understand this time in history.

School and Poetry

Abigail Smith was born in Weymouth, Massachusetts, in 1744. Few girls went to school then. But Abigail's father wanted her to learn. Her mother taught her to read. Abigail taught herself French. And she liked poetry. Through her life, she often repeated poetry from memory.

Marriage to John Adams

In 1764, Abigail married John Adams. He was a young lawyer. They had many ideas to talk about. They had a great friendship and a long marriage. It lasted 54 years.

The couple lived on a farm in Braintree, Massachusetts. They had two children there. Four more were born later.

Letters

Often, John worked far away. When Abigail and John were apart, they wrote letters. They wrote about their lives. And they wrote about their ideas. We have many of the letters today. They help us understand the people and events of the time.

A Move to Boston

John often worked in Boston. In 1768, the family moved there.

This was a difficult time. Some colonists wanted to be free from Britain. Britain did not want the colonies to be free. People were angry. Sometimes there was violence. Abigail saw many important events happen in Boston.

John and Abigail wanted freedom. John became a leader of the colonists. Many other leaders came to their home. Abigail talked with them and discussed the future.

Running the Farm

In 1775, war began between the colonies and Britain. This war was the American Revolution.

Did you know?

Abigail Adams was the wife and the mother of presidents. Her husband, John Adams, was the second U.S. president. Her son John Quincy Adams was the sixth president.

Abigail Adams lived at the Braintree farm during the war. Often, she didn't see John for months. But they still wrote letters. She urged John to work for freedom.

In those days, men usually ran farms and businesses. But John was away from home often. So Abigail ran their farm. It was the best farm in the area.

Women's Rights

In 1776, John and other leaders made plans to form a new nation. Abigail wrote John a letter. She told him to "remember the ladies."[1] She told him that men shouldn't have all the power. She said that women should have rights too. In the 1700s, women in America had few rights. And few men wanted them to have more.

After Abigail and John died, other people read their letters. Abigail became famous. She talked about women's rights when few others gave them a thought.

A New Nation

The colonists won the war. The fighting ended in 1781. Then the Americans started a new nation—the United States. John Adams helped lead the new nation during its first years.

In 1789, George Washington became the first U.S. president. John Adams was the first vice president. In 1797, John became president. So Abigail was First Lady.

Abigail Adams was a busy First Lady. She had many jobs. She took care of her family. She also had many visitors. Sometimes 60 people came in one day. And she was John's best friend. He listened to her ideas.

Final Years

In 1801, John finished his job as president. Abigail and John went back to their farm. Finally, they had time together. But they still had much to do. They had many visitors. And they had a big family with grandchildren.

Abigail and John enjoyed their last years together. In 1818, Abigail died. John died eight years later, in 1826.

Comprehension

Check the answer that completes each sentence correctly.

1. When Abigail Smith was a child,

    _____ a. most girls didn't go to school.

    _____ b. her father kept her out of school.

2. Abigail and John Adams had a long marriage and

    _____ a. only two children.

    _____ b. a good friendship.

3. Many colonists wanted

    _____ a. to make John Adams president.

    _____ b. freedom from Britain.

4. Abigail and John Adams moved to Boston because

    _____ a. it was safer than Braintree.

    _____ b. John often worked there.

5. The colonists fought the American Revolution

    _____ a. to get free from Britain.

    _____ b. to end the violence in Boston.

6. Abigail Adams became First Lady when

    _____ a. George Washington became president.

    _____ b. John Adams became president.

7. After John Adams finished his job as president,
he and Abigail

    _____ a. went back to their farm.

    _____ b. wrote letters about their ideas.

Making Inferences

Read each statement or question. What do you think that Abigail Adams would say? Check your answer.

1. What is needed to make a marriage last?

    _____ a. A wife should always agree with her husband.

    _____ b. A husband and wife must be friends.

2. John traveled too much.

    _____ a. I disagree. He had important work to do.

    _____ b. I agree. There was enough work in Boston.

3. Women need to read and write.

    _____ a. No, women do not need to read to raise children.

    _____ b. Yes, women need to read and write as much as men do.

Vocabulary

Look at these words from the reading. Put a check next to words that you know. Underline words that you don't know yet. Find the words in the reading. Try to guess their meanings.

colonists   poetry   vice president
lawyer   ran   violence

Fill in each blank. Use words from the box.

1. Many _____ wanted America to be free from Britain.

2. The _____ runs the country if the president is too sick.

3. The _____ made Boston dangerous.

4. Abigail Adams _____ the farm when John was away.

5. As a _____, John Adams knew the law.

6. Abigail Adams liked to read _____.

Reading a Time Line

Time lines show events in order on a line. This time line shows events in Abigail Adams's life.

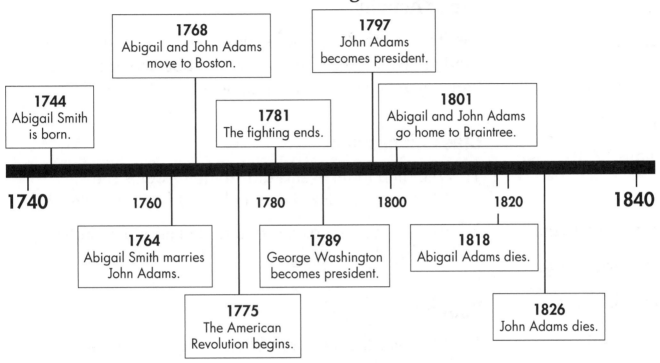

The Life of Abigail Adams

1768 Abigail and John Adams move to Boston.

1797 John Adams becomes president.

1744 Abigail Smith is born.

1781 The fighting ends.

1801 Abigail and John Adams go home to Braintree.

1740   1760   1780   1800   1820   1840

1764 Abigail Smith marries John Adams.

1789 George Washington becomes president.

1818 Abigail Adams dies.

1775 The American Revolution begins.

1826 John Adams dies.

Fill in each blank. Use information from the time line.

1. Abigail Smith and John Adams got married in the year _____.

2. Abigail Smith was _____ years old when she got married.

3. Seven years before the American Revolution began, John and

   Abigail Adams _____.

4. In the American Revolution, the fighting lasted for _____ years.

5. Abigail Adams was _____ years old when she died.

In a letter to John, Abigail Adams wrote, "My pen is always freer than my tongue." [2]

Is it sometimes easier to write about things than to talk about them? Explain.

Connecting Today and Yesterday

Abigail Adams lived through important events. Think about the events during your life. Are they as important? Explain.

Group Activity

The Boston Tea Party happened in 1773. Abigail Adams lived in Boston then. Find out more about the Boston Tea Party. In your group, talk about what you learn.

Class Discussion

1. What important events did Abigail Adams see? What do you think she thought and felt about them?

2. Abigail Adams was married to an important leader. How did this marriage help her learn about events?

Reflections

1. What was the most interesting thing that you read in this lesson?

2. How can you learn more about Abigail Adams?

George Washington

Father of His Country

Pre-Reading Question

Why is George Washington remembered today?

Reading Preview

George Washington was an important leader. First he led the American army in war with Britain. Then he led the new United States in peace.

George Washington

George Washington led the colonial army during the American Revolution. Then he became the first president of the United States.

Early Life

George Washington was born in Virginia on February 22, 1732. He grew up on a plantation. A plantation is a large farm with many workers. As a child and young man, he learned how to run a farm. And he became a great horse rider.

When George was 11 years old, his father died. George did not go to school much after that. But he became good in math. At 16, he became a land surveyor. He measured land for farms and towns. When he was 20, he joined the army. He was a good soldier. Soon he became an officer. In the 1750s, he fought in a war between France and Britain. These countries both had colonies in America. Many battles were fought in the colonies.

Marriage

In 1759, Washington married Martha Custis. They lived on Washington's plantation in Virginia. It was called Mount Vernon. Washington was a skilled farmer. He grew tobacco, and he raised cattle. Slavery was legal then. Slaves worked on his plantation. Later, Washington decided that slavery was wrong. When he died, he left directions to free his slaves. They became free when Martha died.

Washington's Early Public Life

From 1759 to 1774, Washington served in the government of Virginia. During this time, Britain made the colonists pay taxes. Many colonists were angry. They said that the taxes were unfair. They had no power in Britain's government. Britain taxed them, but it did not give them a choice. So representatives from 12 of the 13 colonies had a meeting. Washington came from Virginia. The representatives asked Britain to end the taxes. But Britain did not agree.

The American Revolution

On April 19, 1775, British soldiers went to Concord, Massachusetts. They planned to destroy the colonists' guns. Some colonists fought the British. This battle started the American Revolution. Soon the colonists asked Washington to lead their army.

Leader of the Colonial Army

Washington had a small army, but he trained his men well. They fought in all kinds of weather. Sometimes they were hungry. But the soldiers fought bravely. They liked Washington. He was a good leader.

The colonial army fought the British for six years. Then in 1781, they had a battle at Yorktown. The colonists won. This was the last battle of the war. The United States became a free nation.

The First President

The new nation had 13 states. In 1787, representatives met to write a constitution. They asked Washington to lead the meeting. He helped everyone work together. They wrote the Constitution of the United States.

Then the new country had its first election. They chose Washington as the first president. He wanted to make the new government work for the people. He had much to do.

Washington was elected to a second term in 1792. He did not want a third term. John Adams was elected president in 1796. Washington went home to Mount Vernon in 1797.

Washington's Death

On December 12, 1799, Washington rode his horse through his plantation. It was a cold, snowy day. When he got home, he felt sick. He had a sore throat. Soon it was hard for him to breathe. Two days later, Washington died. He was 67 years old.

Did you know?

Washington refused to take a salary for leading the American army. He took money only for his expenses.

Honoring George Washington

Newspapers reported Washington's death. Many people felt sadness and loss. King William IV of Britain called Washington "the greatest man who ever lived."[1]

In Congress, Representative John Marshall talked about Washington's death. He said, "Our Washington is no more. The hero . . . lives now only in his own great actions, and in the hearts of . . . people."[2]

Comprehension

Read each statement. If it is correct, check *Yes*. If not, check *No*.

Yes   No

_____ _____ 1. Washington grew up on a farm.

_____ _____ 2. Washington's father died when George was young.

_____ _____ 3. Washington freed his slaves when he was president.

_____ _____ 4. The colonists won the battle at Yorktown.

_____ _____ 5. Washington wrote the Constitution by himself.

_____ _____ 6. Washington was president for two terms.

_____ _____ 7. King William IV thought that Washington was a bad leader.

Sequence

Number the events in the correct order.

_____ Washington becomes president.

_____ Colonists fight British soldiers at Concord.

_____ Washington marries Martha Custis.

_____ Washington becomes leader of the colonial army.

_____ The Constitution is written.

Vocabulary

Look at these words from the reading. Put a check next to words that you know. Underline words that you don't know yet. Find the words in the reading. Try to guess their meanings.

constitution   plantation   surveyor
election   representative   term

Choose the answer that completes each sentence correctly.
Write it in the blank.

1. The rules for the government are in the _____.
   constitution/plantation

2. Each state sent _____ to the meeting.
   representatives/surveyors

3. A _____ can tell you the size of a farm.
   representative/surveyor

4. People wanted Washington to serve another _____
   election/term

   as president.

5. Washington grew tobacco on his _____.
   plantation/term

6. _____ was held to choose the president.
   A constitution/An election

Reading a Map

Political maps can show the borders of countries, states, and cities. This political map shows the first 13 states of the United States.

The United States in 1781

Choose the answer that completes each sentence correctly. Write it in the blank. Use information from the map.

1. Yorktown is in _____.
   North Carolina/Virginia

2. Georgia is _____ of New York.
   north/south

3. _____ is the smallest state.
   Rhode Island/Maryland

4. Philadelphia is about _____ from Mount Vernon.
   115 miles/190 miles

5. All of the states are _____ of the Atlantic Ocean.
   east/west

Connecting Today and Yesterday

Washington did many things for the United States. Which is most important today? Why do you think so?

Group Activity

People tell many stories about Washington. Some are true. Some are just stories. Find out more about Washington's life. In your group, talk about what you learn.

Class Discussion

1. Describe George Washington. What kind of person was he?

2. Washington led the country in war. He also led the country in peace. Which job was more important? Explain.

Reflections

1. Can you use anything from George Washington's story in your own life? Explain.

2. How can you learn more about George Washington?

Henry Lee was one of Washington's officers. He said that Washington was "first in war, first in peace, and first in the hearts of his countrymen."[3]

Is this true about George Washington? Why or why not?

Paul Revere

Messenger of the Revolution

Pre-Reading Question

Have you heard of the Boston Tea Party? Explain what you know about it.

Reading Preview

Paul Revere believed in freedom. So he worked to make the colonies free. He risked his life. He carried a warning to the colonial leaders. Then Revere watched the American Revolution begin.

Paul Revere

The American Revolution began in Massachusetts in April 1775. Paul Revere was at the center of the action.

Early Life

Paul Revere's father came from France. His name was Apollos Rivoire. In America, he changed it to Paul Revere. He was a skilled worker in gold and silver. He made plates, candlesticks, and many other items. In 1734, his son was born in Boston, Massachusetts. He was named Paul Revere also. His father taught young Paul to work with metals.

When his father died, Paul took over the family business. He was just 19. But he did good work. Today, people collect Revere's work. It is finely made and costly.

In 1757, Revere married Sarah Orne. They had eight children. But 16 years later, Sarah died. Soon after, in 1773, Revere married Rachel Walker. They also had eight children.

A Public Life

The 1770s were hard times in the colonies. Britain made the colonists pay taxes. Many colonists were angry. They didn't have anyone in Britain to speak for them. They didn't have a choice.

Because of these taxes, some colonists wanted their own country. They wanted to make their own laws. They talked about a rebellion. Revere agreed with them. He became one of their leaders in Boston.

The Boston Tea Party

Tea was one of the items that Britain taxed. It was a small tax. But the colonists thought it was unfair.

In 1773, three ships sat in Boston Harbor. They were loaded with tea. One night, colonists dressed like American Indians. They threw the tea into the water. Revere helped lead the colonists. This event is called the Boston Tea Party.

Britain was angry at the colonists. Its leaders made new laws. These laws hurt business in the colonies. The conflict between the colonies and Britain got worse.

The Midnight Ride

Some colonists prepared for war. They collected guns and supplies. Groups of men trained to fight. These groups were called militia.

In 1775, the colonists heard news. British soldiers planned to go to Concord, a town near Boston. They wanted to destroy the militia's guns. And they wanted to arrest some of the colonists' leaders. But no one knew when.

On April 18, the British started for Concord. Revere heard the news. He and other messengers rode through the night. They risked their lives. But they warned the colonists in time.

A small group of militia gathered. They met the British in the towns of Lexington and Concord. They fought there. The battles started the American Revolution. Revere was at Lexington that morning. He watched the Revolution begin.

The War

Revere became a soldier in the war. Most of the time, he stayed in Boston. He helped defend the city.

But Revere wanted to do more. Finally, he was sent to fight in a battle. He was in charge of the cannon. The battle went badly. Some people blamed Revere for the defeat. Later, the army said that he did his best.

The Last Years

After the war, Revere went back to his business. As always, he worked hard. He made fine silverware. And he opened other businesses. He made bells for churches and cannons for ships. His businesses did well. He made his sons and then his grandsons part of the business.

Revere died in 1818. He is remembered as a patriot. But he is remembered best for his midnight ride.

Did you know?

Before the Revolution, Revere's silver business was slow. So he also worked as a dentist. He cleaned people's teeth. And he fixed false teeth.

Comprehension

Check the answer that completes each sentence correctly.

1. Paul Revere's father taught Paul

   _____ a. to make furniture.

   _____ b. to make things from silver and gold.

2. Paul Revere had

   _____ a. eight children altogether.

   _____ b. 16 children altogether.

3. For the Boston Tea Party, colonists dressed like

   _____ a. American Indians.

   _____ b. militia.

4. The fighting at Lexington and Concord

   _____ a began the Boston Tea Party.

   _____ b. began the American Revolution.

5. Late one night, Revere rode to warn

   _____ a. the British.

   _____ b. the colonists.

6. During the American Revolution, Revere

   _____ a. was a soldier in Boston.

   _____ b. did not fight.

7. After the American Revolution, Revere

   _____ a. went back to his businesses.

   _____ b. married Rachel Walker.

Cause and Effect

Read each statement. Decide why this happened. Check the reason.

1. Paul Revere took over the family business because

   _____ a. his father died.

   _____ b. his father joined the militia.

2. The colonists didn't want to pay taxes because

   _____ a. they thought that the taxes were unfair.

   _____ b. business was bad in the colonies.

3. The colonists held the Boston Tea Party because

   _____ a. they were angry about American Indians.

   _____ b. they were angry about taxes.

4. British soldiers went to Concord because

   _____ a. they wanted to destroy the militia's guns.

   _____ b. they wanted to fight the militia.

Vocabulary

Look at these words from the reading. Put a check next to words that you know. Underline words that you don't know yet. Find the words in the reading. Try to guess their meanings.

business	militia	taxes
messenger	rebellion	

Fill in each blank. Use words from the box.

1. Revere started a _____. He made bells and cannons.

2. No one likes to pay _____.

3. The colonists planned a _____ against Britain.

4. The _____ trained to fight the British soldiers.

5. Revere was a _____. He warned the colonists.

Reading a Map

Political maps can show where towns and other places are. This political map shows Paul Revere's ride. It includes the places that he visited.

Paul Revere's Midnight Ride

Choose the answer that completes each sentence correctly.
Write it in the blank. Use information from the map.

1. Revere crossed Boston Harbor in a boat. He landed at _____.
   Charlestown/Menotomy

2. Both the British and Revere reached _____.
   Lexington/Medford

3. Boston is about _____ from Concord.
   20 miles/75 miles

4. Revere went _____ when he left Boston.
   east/west

5. _____ was the last town that Revere reached.
   Lexington/Concord

The poet Henry Wadsworth Longfellow helped make Revere a hero. He wrote an exciting poem called "Paul Revere's Ride." The poem made the midnight ride famous. But it had some facts wrong.

Was it OK for Longfellow to change some events? Or are facts more important than an exciting story? Explain.

Connecting Today and Yesterday

Paul Revere wasn't very important in the American Revolution. Should people remember him today? Why or why not?

Group Activity

Paul Revere was not the only messenger on April 18, 1775. William Dawes and Dr. Samuel Prescott also rode to warn the colonists. Learn about Dawes and Prescott. In your group, talk about what they did.

Class Discussion

1. What did Revere do on his midnight ride? Why was it important?

2. When Revere died, a newspaper called him "honorable and useful."[1] Does this description fit? Why or why not?

Reflections

1. What was the most interesting thing that you read in this lesson?

2. How can you learn more about Paul Revere?

Noah Webster

Author of America's First Dictionary

THE AMERICAN SPELLING BOOK, CONTAINING THE RUDIMENTS OF THE ENGLISH LANGUAGE FOR THE USE OF SCHOOLS IN THE UNITED STATES. BY NOAH WEBSTER, ESQ.

THE REVISED IMPRESSION, WITH THE LATEST CORRECTIONS.

MIDDLETOWN, CONN.
PUBLISHED BY WILLIAM H. NILES.
STEREOTYPED BY A. CHANDLER.
1830.

Pre-Reading Question

What do you know about Webster's dictionary?

Reading Preview

Noah Webster wrote schoolbooks and dictionaries. Schools across the United States used his books. These books helped change the English language in America.

Noah Webster

Noah Webster wrote books that taught children to read and spell. He wrote the first dictionary of American English. He helped change the American language.

Early Life

Noah Webster's family came to America in the 1630s. They were some of the first Europeans in Connecticut. They were mostly farmers. His father was also a farmer.

Noah was born in West Hartford, Connecticut, in 1758. As a child, he worked on the farm. He went to school when he wasn't working. His parents were not rich, but they sent him to college. He went to Yale in 1774.

Then the American Revolution started. Webster and his classmates formed a militia. Twice he marched off to war. Webster finally finished school in 1778.

A Teacher

Webster studied art, science, and literature at Yale. He didn't learn a job. When he left Yale, he went home to the farm. But he wasn't happy there, so he became a teacher. In 1782, he opened his own grade school. Webster looked at schoolbooks. They were written in Britain. They taught the language and culture of Britain.

Webster didn't like these schoolbooks. Language was different in the United States. And he wanted children to learn about their country.

The *American Spelling Book*

Webster began to write his own schoolbooks. He published the first one in 1783. He called it the *American Spelling Book.* It taught spelling of American English. Schools used it for more than 100 years.

The Living Language

In the old British spelling books, language didn't change. Words were spelled the same as 200 years before.

But Webster said that language changed all the time. He taught modern spellings. He made changes like these:

Old British Spelling	Modern American Spelling
favour	favor
publick	public
centre	center

Webster also wanted all Americans to spell words the same way. Until then, people spelled words the way they sounded. People in different parts of the United States spoke differently. So they spelled words differently. Webster's spelling book taught one spelling for each word.

More New Books

Webster then wrote the *American Grammar.* It taught rules for using English. He also wrote the *American Reader.* It taught reading and literature. People liked Webster's books. Soon schools across the country used them.

Webster's First Dictionary

Next, Webster wrote a dictionary. Until then, most Americans used British dictionaries. But these books didn't have American words. They listed British spellings and pronunciations.

Webster published his first dictionary in 1806. It was a small book. It listed American words. It had just one spelling and one pronunciation for each word.

The Second Dictionary

The next year, Webster started his major work. He spent the next 21 years writing *An American Dictionary of the English Language.* He finished it in 1828. It had more than 70,000 word entries.

Did you know?
A small dictionary has about 60,000 entries. A normal desk dictionary has about 150,000 entries. The largest dictionary of American English has about 470,000 entries.

Webster was 70 years old when he finished this dictionary. But he wanted to make it even better. He wanted it to have the latest words and spellings. He started work on a new dictionary. He worked on it until he died in 1843.

Millions of Books

Webster's books lived on. Millions were sold during his lifetime. Millions more were sold after his death. His spelling book was used in schools until 1936.

And people still talk about "Webster's." Now Webster's name means any dictionary.

Comprehension

Read each statement. If it is correct, check *Yes*. If not, check *No*.

Yes　**No**

_____　_____　1. As a child, Webster went to school when he wasn't working on the farm.

_____　_____　2. At Yale, Webster studied teaching and math.

_____　_____　3. British spelling books taught American English.

_____　_____　4. The *American Spelling Book* taught reading and literature.

_____　_____　5. Webster thought that language changed over time.

_____　_____　6. Webster's dictionaries gave the American pronunciations of words.

_____　_____　7. Webster wanted all Americans to spell words the same way.

Cause and Effect

Read each statement. Decide why this happened. Check the reason.

1. Webster went back to his father's farm after college because

    _____ a. he wanted to be a farmer.

    _____ b. he did not learn a job in college.

2. Americans spelled words differently in places because

    _____ a. they spoke different languages.

    _____ b. they pronounced words differently.

3. After 1828, Webster began work on a new dictionary because

    _____ a. he wanted to add the newest words and spellings.

    _____ b. the 1828 dictionary had many mistakes.

Vocabulary

Look at these words from the reading. Put a check next to words that you know. Underline words that you don't know yet. Find the words in the reading. Try to guess their meanings.

culture	entries	pronunciation
dictionary	modern	published

Fill in each blank. Use words from the box.

1. Webster wrote a dictionary, and then he _____ it.

2. People look in a _____ to learn the meanings of words.

3. The way a group of people thinks and acts is their _____.

4. To learn how to say a word, look up the _____.

5. Webster's dictionary had more than 70,000 word _____.

6. Webster used up-to-date, _____ spellings.

Reading a Time Line

Time lines show events in order on a line. This time line shows events in Noah Webster's life.

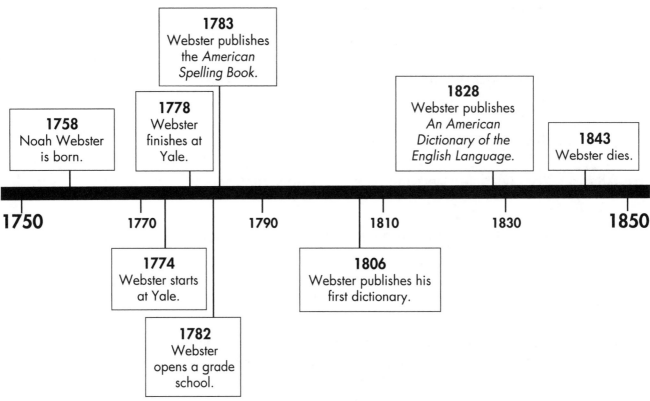

The Life of Noah Webster

Fill in each blank. Use information from the time line.

1. Noah Webster was born in the year _____.

2. Webster was _____ years old when he started at Yale.

3. The *American Spelling Book* was published 9 years after Webster

   _____.

4. *An American Dictionary of the English Language* was published

   _____ years after Webster's first dictionary.

5. Webster was _____ years old when he died.

Connecting Today and Yesterday

Noah Webster wrote a dictionary of American English. It helped people in the United States to speak and spell the same way. Is this important today? Why or why not?

Group Activity

The *American Spelling Book* is still published. Get the book from the library or find it on the Internet. Read some parts of it with your group. Talk about what it teaches. Is it still useful?

Class Discussion

1. Webster thought that the United States needed one language. He believed that everyone should pronounce and spell words the same way. He believed that this would make the country stronger. Do you agree? Why or why not?

2. Noah Webster and his books are still famous. Why? Explain your opinion.

Reflections

1. Can you use anything from Noah Webster's story in your own life? Explain.

2. How can you learn more about Noah Webster?

Henry Ward Beecher was a reformer and preacher in the 19th century. He wrote, "All words are pegs to hang ideas on."[1]

Do you think that Webster would agree with Beecher? Do you agree? Why or why not?

Ulysses S. Grant

"He was the truest as well as the bravest man that ever lived."

—James Longstreet, Confederate general and friend[1]

Pre-Reading Questions

What do you know about the U.S. Civil War?
Why was it fought?

Reading Preview

Ulysses S. Grant led the Union army in the Civil War. More than 600,000 soldiers died. It almost destroyed the United States. But Grant was a great commander. He helped the Union win that war. Later, he led the United States as president.

Ulysses S. Grant

Ulysses S. Grant was commander of the Union army. He helped the Union win the U.S. Civil War, which kept the country together. After the war, he became president of the United States.

Early Life

Ulysses S. Grant was born in 1822 in Ohio. He went to local schools.

Horses were important to Grant all his life. He learned to ride when he was very small. He became a famous local rider. He even tamed horses. When he was 9, farmers asked him to train their horses.

Start of a Military Career

At 17, Grant entered West Point. This military school trains army officers. Grant didn't want to go to West Point. He wanted to be a farmer, not a soldier. But his father made him go.

Grant finished West Point in 1843. He was made an officer. The army sent him to St. Louis, Missouri. He planned to leave the army after four years. Then he met Julia Dent in St. Louis. He married her in 1848. And he stayed in the army.

In 1846, a war began between the United States and Mexico. Grant fought in several battles.

In 1854, Grant quit the army. He wanted to spend time with his family. He had two children by then. Two more were born later. He went back to St. Louis and became a farmer.

The Civil War

The Civil War started in 1861. The war was between states in the North and in the South. Eleven Southern states left the United States. They formed their own country. They called it the Confederacy.

The Northern states didn't want the Southern states to leave. They fought to keep them in the United States. The Northern states were called the Union.

Did you know?

Grant's father named him Hiram Ulysses Grant. But West Point made a mistake with his name. It was written "Ulysses S. Grant." From then on, Grant used that name.

General in the Union Army

When the Civil War began, Grant joined the army again. He led a small number of soldiers at first. But he won an important battle. Then Abraham Lincoln made Grant a general. Grant had more soldiers. He led them to more victories.

Commander of the Union Army

The Civil War was a terrible war. It split up families and friends. Farms were ruined. Businesses were destroyed. And about 620,000 soldiers died. The war lasted from 1861 to 1865.

General Grant was the Union's best leader. In 1864, Lincoln made him the commander of the whole Union army. Grant led his army in bloody battles. Thousands of soldiers died. But he won battles. Finally in 1865, Grant forced the Southern commander to surrender, or give up.

President of the United States

The Civil War was over. But the nation was still divided. It needed a strong leader. Many people turned to Grant once more. He was a great hero. He helped save the United States. Now they wanted him to be president.

Grant was president from 1869 to 1877. He was not a great president. Those were difficult years. The United States had many problems. And Grant could not solve them.

The Final Years

Grant stopped being president in 1877. For two years, his family traveled. They went to Europe and around the world. Later, they lived in New York City. Grant went into business, but he lost his money. He also got sick. He was dying.

Grant needed to support his family. He decided to write a memoir about the Civil War. He finished his book, *Personal Memoirs of U.S. Grant,* in 1885. He died a few days later.

After his death, his book was very successful. It took care of all his family's needs.

Comprehension

Check the answer that completes each sentence correctly.

1. Ulysses S. Grant went to West Point to learn to

    _____ a. ride horses.

    _____ b. be a soldier.

2. Grant first went to war during

    _____ a. the war with Mexico.

    _____ b. the Civil War.

3. The Civil War was fought between

    _____ a. the Northern and Southern states.

    _____ b. Mexico and the United States.

4. Lincoln made Grant commander of

    _____ a. the Confederate army.

    _____ b. the Union army.

5. During the Civil War,

    _____ a. Grant left the army.

    _____ b. 620,000 soldiers died.

6. After the Civil War, people of the United States

    _____ a. were still divided.

    _____ b. wanted Lincoln to be president.

7. Grant wrote his memoir

    _____ a. to become president.

    _____ b. to make money for his family.

Sequence

Number the events in the correct order.

_____ The Civil War begins.

_____ Grant marries Julia Dent.

_____ Grant becomes president.

_____ The war with Mexico begins.

_____ Lincoln makes Grant commander of the Union army.

Vocabulary

Look at these words from the reading. Put a check next to words that you know. Underline words that you don't know yet. Find the words in the reading. Try to guess their meanings.

commander   memoir   officer
famous   military   soldier

Choose the answer that completes each sentence correctly. Write it in the blank.

1. _____ leads soldiers in war.

A memoir/An officer

2. Every _____ learns to fight.

famous/soldier

3. Grant wrote a _____ about the Civil War.

commander/memoir

4. Grant was the _____ of the army during the war.

commander/military

5. West Point is a _____ school.

military/soldier

6. Many people knew about Grant. He was _____.

famous/memoir

Reading a Map

Political maps can show borders of countries, states, and cities. This map shows the United States at the beginning of the Civil War. Some states stayed in the Union. Others formed the Confederacy. Look at the key to see which states were in each group.

The U.S. at the Beginning of the Civil War

Read each statement. If it is correct, check *Yes*. If not, check *No*. Use information from the map.

Yes   No

____ ____ 1. The Confederacy had 11 states.

____ ____ 2. Ohio was a Confederate state.

____ ____ 3. Texas was west of all the other Confederate states.

____ ____ 4. The territories were part of the Confederacy.

____ ____ 5. Two Union states were west of the territories.

In describing Grant, Abraham Lincoln said, "He has the grit of a bull-dog! Once let him get his 'teeth' in, and nothing can shake him off." [2]

Do you think this describes a good military officer? Why or why not?

Connecting Today and Yesterday

Think about today's leaders. Are any of them like Ulysses S. Grant? Explain.

Group Activity

Learn more about the causes of the Civil War. Why did some Southern states want to leave the United States? In your group, discuss what you learn.

Class Discussion

1. What kind of person was Ulysses S. Grant?
2. Ulysses S. Grant was a military leader. Then he became president. Do you think military leaders make good leaders of countries? Why or why not?

Reflections

1. What was the most interesting thing that you read in this lesson?
2. How can you learn more about Ulysses S. Grant?

Sojourner Truth

"The Lord gave me Sojourner, because I was to travel up an' down the land, . . . and the Lord gave me Truth, because I was to declare the truth to the people."

—Sojourner Truth,
on how she got her name[1]

Pre-Reading Question

What do you know about slavery in the United States?

Reading Preview

Sojourner Truth was born a slave, but she became free. She spoke out against slavery. She also spoke for the rights of women. She helped many Americans gain their rights.

Sojourner Truth

Sojourner Truth was born a slave. When she became free, she told many people about slavery. She also supported women's rights. People listened to her. She helped change the United States.

Hard to Forget

People said that Sojourner Truth was a wonderful speaker. Her voice was very low. It was powerful and strong. She chose her words perfectly. In just a few words, she thrilled her listeners. And she sang beautifully.

Truth stood almost six feet tall. She was thin. But she was strong from her years of hard work as a slave.

Born a Slave

Sojourner Truth was born a slave in New York State. A Dutch family owned her. So Dutch was her first language. She later learned to speak English. But she never lost her Dutch accent.

Truth was born in about 1797. No one knows exactly when. People didn't keep careful records about slaves. She was born somewhere in Ulster County. Her parents named her Isabella Baumfree.

Truth lived the typical life of a Northern slave. She was separated from her parents at age 11. She was sold to another owner. She suffered abuse. She carried the scars from a beating all her life.

Free at Last

New York State began to free slaves on July 4, 1827. But Truth didn't wait. In 1826, she walked away. Truth had five children. She carried her youngest with her. She didn't go far. She stayed with a family that lived nearby.

During this time, Truth became religious. She helped start a Methodist church. Late in 1828, she moved to New York City. She stayed there for about 15 years. Her faith grew stronger. She became a preacher.

A New Name

In 1843, Isabella changed her name to Sojourner Truth. Then she left New York. She walked and preached along the way. After several months, Truth reached Northampton, Massachusetts. A group there opposed slavery. Some members worked actively to end it. Truth joined the group.

The Narrative of Sojourner Truth

The group at Northampton broke up in 1846. But Truth stayed there until the mid-1850s. At this time, she told her story to a friend. She told about her life as a slave. She explained her religious faith. Her friend wrote the story for her. (Truth never learned to read or write.) Truth published the book as *The Narrative of Sojourner Truth.*

Fight against Slavery

Many people in the United States opposed slavery. Truth met many of the leaders at Northampton. She began to preach against slavery.

Truth spoke in meetings across the country. She said that slavery was wrong. She also talked about her religious beliefs. It was a powerful message. She spoke simply. But she got everyone's attention. She made people listen.

The Civil War ended slavery in the United States. Truth worked to help the freed slaves. She raised money for food and clothing. She tried to get schools for them.

Women's Rights

Truth also talked about women's rights. In the 1800s, women had few rights. They could not vote. Few went to school. Married women could not own property. Married women's wages belonged to their husbands.

Truth became famous for her speeches and her leadership. The fight went on for many years. Slowly, women gained their rights. They won the right to vote in 1920. Other rights came even more slowly.

Did you know?

In the early 1800s, black women had almost no rights. Yet Sojourner Truth went to court. She asked a judge to free her son, Peter. She won. She was the first black woman to sue and win in a U.S. court.

The Final Years

In the 1860s and 1870s, Truth had several serious illnesses. But she kept working. She traveled and gave speeches.

Truth lived in Battle Creek, Michigan, with two of her daughters. Another child and grandchildren lived nearby. In her final years, she stayed close to home. Sojourner Truth died in 1883.

Comprehension

Read each statement. If it is correct, check *Yes*. If not, check *No*.

Yes   No

____   ____   1. Truth was famous for her skill at public speaking.

____   ____   2. Truth got the name *Sojourner* from her first owner.

____   ____   3. At age 11, Truth walked away from her owner.

____   ____   4. Friends in Northampton taught Truth to read.

____   ____   5. The Civil War ended slavery in the United States.

____   ____   6. Truth dictated *The Narrative of Sojourner Truth.*

____   ____   7. Women won the right to vote during Truth's lifetime.

Making Inferences

Read each statement or question. What do you think that Sojourner Truth would say? Check your answer.

1. Some slave owners are good people.

   ____ a. No, good people do not keep slaves.

   ____ b. Yes, some slave owners care about their slaves.

2. Why should we build schools for the freed slaves?

   ____ a. They need help to get started.

   ____ b. They don't want help from white people.

3. Not everyone needs faith.

   ____ a. I agree. People do not need faith to help others.

   ____ b. I disagree. Faith gives people strength.

Vocabulary

Look at these words from the reading. Put a check next to words that you know. Underline words that you don't know yet. Find the words in the reading. Try to guess their meanings.

abuse	broke up	rights
accent	preacher	slavery

Fill in each blank. Use words from the box.

1. She had an _____. She spoke differently from other people.

2. Truth opposed _____. She said that it was wrong to own

   another person.

3. She remembered the pain and _____ of slavery all her life.

4. When Truth became a _____, she spoke about her religious faith.

5. The couple was always fighting, and soon they _____.

6. Women fought for their _____.

Reading a Chart

Charts show information in rows and columns. This chart shows the number of people in the United States for different years. It shows three groups: slaves, free persons, and total population. Total population is all the people in the United States. It includes both slaves and free persons.

Population of the United States, 1800–1860

Year	Slaves	Free Persons	Total Population
1800	887,612	4,349,019	5,236,631
1810	1,130,781	5,905,728	7,036,509
1820	1,529,012	8,557,003	10,086,015
1830	1,987,428	10,798,500	12,785,928
1840	2,482,556	14,536,335	17,018,891
1850	3,200,600	19,853,552	23,054,152
1860	3,950,528	27,233,216	31,183,744

Choose the answer that completes each sentence correctly. Write it in the blank. Use information from the chart.

1. In 1800, _____ people lived in the United States.
   5,236,631/887,612

2. Between 1800 and 1860, the slave population got _____.
   smaller/larger

3. In 1860, there were about _____ more slaves than in 1800.
   3 million/4 million

4. The U.S. population grew most in the years _____.
   1800–1810/1850–1860

Connecting Today and Yesterday

Sojourner Truth preached about the wrongs of slavery. She talked about women's rights. Is her work still important to people today? Why or why not?

Group Activity

In December 1851, Sojourner Truth spoke at the Women's Rights Convention in Akron, Ohio. In her speech, she asked many times, "Ain't I a woman?" The speech became famous. Today, people call it "Ain't I a Woman?" Find a copy on the Internet or in the library. Read it, and discuss it in your group.

Class Discussion

1. What kind of person was Sojourner Truth? Why did people listen to her so carefully?

2. Imagine that you could talk to Sojourner Truth. What questions would you ask her? What do you think she might say?

Reflections

1. Can you use anything from Sojourner Truth's story in your own life? Explain.

2. How can you learn more about Sojourner Truth?

At a Women's Rights Convention, Truth said, "If women want any rights more than they's got, why don't they just take them, and not be talking about it?"[2]

What do you think she meant? Do you agree?

Thomas Edison

Master Inventor of Menlo Park

Pre-Reading Question

Have any modern inventions changed your life? If yes, describe how.

Reading Preview

Thomas Edison was one of the greatest U.S. inventors. He invented many everyday things, such as the lightbulb and motion pictures. His inventions brought great changes to the United States. Many of them are still used today.

Thomas Edison

Thomas Edison was a famous U.S. inventor. He created machines to store and play sounds. He invented lightbulbs and motion pictures too.

Many Inventions

During the 1800s, new inventions brought great changes to the United States. Thomas Edison helped make these changes possible. He invented many new machines. And he made others better. We still use some of his inventions.

Early Life

Edison was born in 1847 in Milan, Ohio. He went to public school for a short time. But he wasn't interested. So his mother taught him at home. She was a schoolteacher.

As a young child, Edison liked to experiment. When he was about 6, he experimented with fire. It got out of control. He burned down his father's barn.

A Young Hero

At 12, Edison started his first job. He sold newspapers on a train. Soon, he set up his own newspaper. He wrote and printed the newspaper on the train.

One day, Edison was standing beside the train tracks. He saw a small child on the tracks. A train was coming. Edison pulled the child to safety just in time.

The child's father worked on a telegraph. He rewarded Edison. He taught Edison how to use the telegraph. Edison became a telegrapher. He was 16. It was a dull job. But Edison was interested in the telegraph. He wanted to know how everything worked.

Menlo Park

In 1871, Edison decided to be an inventor. He opened a lab. He made his first big invention in 1874. It was an improvement to the telegraph. It sent four messages at one time. Earlier, telegraphs sent only one message at a time. He sold the invention. This was Edison's start.

Edison moved his lab to Menlo Park, New Jersey, in 1876. He hired people to help him. Edison loved inventing. He worked 16 hours a day.

Edison wanted to make an invention every two weeks. And he wanted to make a major invention every three months. He almost met this goal.

Phonographs

One of Edison's biggest inventions was the phonograph. He invented it in 1877. It recorded sounds and played them back. Later, Edison recorded music for phonographs. Phonographs were used for more than 100 years.

Electric Lightbulb

Edison's greatest invention came in 1879. It was the lightbulb. He also invented an entire system to go with it. He invented ways to make electricity. He invented wires to take the electricity to houses. He invented parts for lamps that used lightbulbs.

In 1882, Edison put his first electric system in part of New York City. It lit 25 buildings. Soon, other people used his system. The United States had electric lights.

A Bigger Laboratory

Electric lights were a great success. So Edison built a bigger lab. It was in West Orange, New Jersey. There, he created new inventions. One was motion pictures.

First, he invented a camera to take moving pictures. Then he made a machine to show the pictures. Finally, Edison began making movies. He opened a movie studio at his lab.

Final Years

Edison made more than 1,000 inventions in his life. He died in West Orange in 1931. Thousands of people came to say good-bye. To honor him, many Americans turned off their lights at 10:00 p.m. on October 22, 1931.

Comprehension

Check the answer that completes each sentence correctly.

1. Edison left public school to

   _____ a. get a job on a train.

   _____ b. study at home.

2. Edison's first job was

   _____ a. working as a telegrapher.

   _____ b. selling newspapers.

3. As a teenager, Edison

   _____ a. saved a child.

   _____ b. invented the lightbulb.

4. As an inventor, Edison

   _____ a. worked 16 hours a day.

   _____ b. worked by himself.

5. Edison set up his first electric system in

   _____ a. West Orange, New Jersey.

   _____ b. New York City.

6. Edison's motion picture studio was in

   _____ a. West Orange, New Jersey.

   _____ b. Menlo Park, New Jersey.

7. On October 22, 1931,

   _____ a. Edison turned on the first electric lights in New York City.

   _____ b. people turned off their lights to honor Edison.

Sequence

Number the events in the correct order.

_____ Edison invents the lightbulb.

_____ Edison prints his own newspaper.

_____ Edison becomes a telegrapher.

_____ Edison opens a lab in West Orange.

_____ Edison invents the motion picture camera.

_____ Edison invents the phonograph.

Vocabulary

Look at these words from the reading. Put a check next to words that you know. Underline words that you don't know yet. Find the words in the reading. Try to guess their meanings.

electricity   inventor   motion picture
invention   lab   studio

Choose the answer that completes each sentence correctly.
Write it in the blank.

1. Many people enjoy watching a _____.
   _{motion picture/studio}

2. Edison used _____ to light his lightbulbs.
   _{invention/electricity}

3. Actors worked at the _____.
   _{studio/lab}

4. Edison was a great _____.
   _{inventor/invention}

5. The lightbulb was Edison's greatest _____.
   _{inventor/invention}

6. Edison tried out new ideas in his _____.
   _{invention/lab}

Reading a Chart

Charts show information in rows and columns. This chart lists inventions, inventors, and the dates of the inventions.

Some American Inventions and Their Inventors

Invention	Inventor	Date Invented
safety pin	Walter Hunt	1849
elevator	Elisha Graves Otis	1852
typewriter	Christopher Sholes	1867
telephone	Alexander Graham Bell	1876
zipper	Whitcomb L. Judson	1893
windshield wipers	Mary Anderson	1903
airplane	Wilbur and Orville Wright	1903
air conditioning	W. H. Carrier	1911

Choose the answer that completes each sentence correctly.
Write it in the blank. Use information from the chart.

1. _____ invented air conditioning.
   W. H. Carrier/Walter Hunt

2. Windshield wipers were invented in _____.
   1903/1911

3. Whitcomb L. Judson invented the _____.
   safety pin/zipper

4. The airplane was invented _____ after the typewriter.
   36 years/52 years

5. The _____ was invented in 1876.
   telephone/elevator

Edison said, "I owe my success to the fact that I never had a clock in my workroom."[1]

What does this say about Edison? Do you think it is good advice for other people?

Connecting Today and Yesterday

Edison's inventions changed life in the United States. Have any inventions during your lifetime been as important? Explain.

Group Activity

Imagine that you could talk to Thomas Edison. What questions would you ask? What do you think he would answer? Plan a discussion in your group. Then role-play it.

Class Discussion

1. How did the lightbulb change the way people live?
2. Think about Edison's childhood. Did it suggest what he would become?

Reflections

1. What is the most interesting thing that you read in this lesson?
2. How can you learn more about Thomas Edison?

Jane Addams

"I do not believe that women are better than men. We have not . . . done many unholy things that men have done; but . . . we have not had the chance."

—*Jane Addams*[1]

Pre-Reading Questions

How can someone help other people have a better life? Can one person change the world?

Reading Preview

Jane Addams worked all her life to help people. She started a home in Chicago to help immigrants and working people. She worked for the rights of women. She also worked for peace.

Jane Addams

Jane Addams worked to improve the lives of immigrants and poor people. She also worked for peace and for women's rights.

Early Life

Jane Addams was born in 1860 in Cedarville, Illinois. When she was about 3, her mother died. Jane became very close to her father.

Addams was born with a problem in her back. She couldn't do some things. Later, doctors did surgery. They almost fixed her back. But she always bent over a little.

Addams finished college in 1882. Then she started medical school. She wanted to be a doctor. But she had to quit. She had health problems. And her father died at this time.

Life at Hull House

Addams took time to choose what to do. She traveled, studied, and wrote. She and a friend, Ellen Starr, went to Europe. They saw many problems in the world. They decided to work for reform.

In 1889, Addams and Starr leased a large house in Chicago, Illinois. They called it Hull House. Addams lived and worked there for the rest of her life.

Hull House was in an industrial area. Many immigrants lived in the neighborhood. There were people from Italy, Russia, Ireland, Germany, Greece, and other countries. They were mostly poor, hardworking people.

Center of a Community

Addams, Starr, and other people worked at Hull House. They gave services to the neighborhood. They helped care for children of working parents. They cared for sick people. They held classes for children and adults. They had a library and swimming pool. They helped people find jobs. People gathered at Hull House. They depended on it. Hull House became the center of the community.

Beyond Hull House

Addams's work went beyond Hull House. She worked for many kinds of reform. For example, many parents worked. Older children spent their time on the street. Some broke the law. They were sent to adult courts. Addams helped get children's courts started.

Addams also worked to have childhood sicknesses studied. She helped get children to stay in school. And she worked to get more classrooms and books for students.

Women's Rights

Before 1920, U.S. women did not have the right to vote. Addams believed women needed this right. She said women and men had different views. They worried about different things. Women's ideas and leadership would make the United States better. So Addams worked hard for women's rights. She gave speeches, and she wrote books and essays.

Peacemaker

In 1914, World War I started. Many countries in Europe went to war. Millions of soldiers died. The United States stayed out of the war at first. But in 1917, it entered the war.

Addams said that war did not solve problems. Instead, it created them. War destroyed people, homes, and nations. So she spoke out against it. She joined international groups to work for peace. In 1919, she became president of the Women's International League for Peace and Freedom.

Nobel Prize Winner

Many people were angry with Addams. They thought that the war was right. They said that Addams was not loyal. But many other people respected her. In 1931, she received the Nobel Peace Prize. This prize is given each year to someone who has worked hard for peace.

Did you know?

Hull House once had 13 buildings. Most were torn down in the 1960s. But the work of Hull House continues. Today, it has community centers and programs around Chicago.

Final Respect

The Nobel Prize is presented in Oslo, Norway. But Addams was sick and could not go. She was never really well again. She died in 1935.

Addams's body was placed in Hull House. About 50,000 people came to say good-bye. Leaders of many nations sent messages. The *New York Times* called her "perhaps, the world's best-known and best-loved woman."[2]

Comprehension

Read each statement. If it is correct, check *Yes*. If not, check *No*.

Yes   No

_____ _____ 1. Addams finished medical school.

_____ _____ 2. When Addams was in Europe, she decided to work for reform.

_____ _____ 3. Immigrants from many countries lived near Hull House.

_____ _____ 4. Hull House helped adults as well as children.

_____ _____ 5. Addams thought that women should have the right to vote.

_____ _____ 6. Addams believed that the United States was right to enter World War I.

_____ _____ 7. Addams died before she got the Nobel Prize.

Cause and Effect

Read each statement. Decide why this happened. Check the reason.

1. Jane Addams left medical school because

    _____ a. she went to Europe to study.

    _____ b. she became ill.

2. Hull House became a center for the community because

    _____ a. it helped people.

    _____ b. Addams worked for international peace.

3. Addams helped start courts for children because

    _____ a. children spent time on the streets.

    _____ b. children who broke the law went to adult courts.

4. Addams was given the Nobel Peace Prize because

    _____ a. she spoke out against war.

    _____ b. she started Hull House.

Vocabulary

Look at these words from the reading. Put a check next to words that you know. Underline words that you don't know yet. Find the words in the reading. Try to guess their meanings.

immigrants   international   reform
industrial   peace

Fill in each blank. Use words from the box.

1. Both parents were _____. They came from Bosnia.

2. Addams opposed war and worked for _____.

3. Many companies were in the _____ area.

4. People came from 20 countries. It was an _____ meeting.

5. Addams wanted _____ so that children could go to children's courts.

Reading a Time Line

Time lines show events in order on a line. This time line shows events in Jane Addams's life.

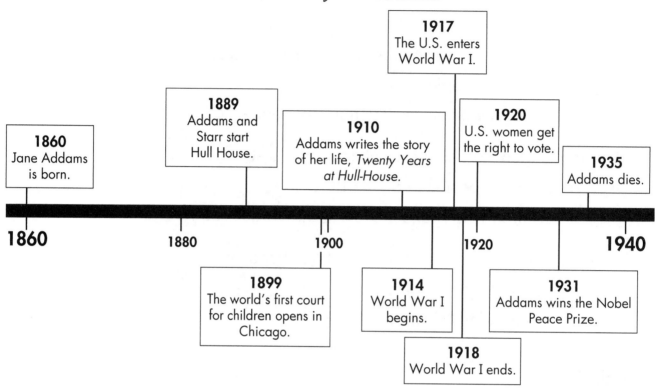

The Life of Jane Addams

1860 Jane Addams is born.

1889 Addams and Starr start Hull House.

1910 Addams writes the story of her life, *Twenty Years at Hull-House.*

1917 The U.S. enters World War I.

1920 U.S. women get the right to vote.

1935 Addams dies.

1860   1880   1900   1920   1940

1899 The world's first court for children opens in Chicago.

1914 World War I begins.

1918 World War I ends.

1931 Addams wins the Nobel Peace Prize.

Fill in each blank. Use information from the time line.

1. The first court for children was started in _____.

2. World War I lasted for _____ years.

3. Addams was _____ years old when she got the right to vote.

4. Addams got the Nobel Peace Prize in _____.

5. Addams was _____ years old when she died.

Connecting Today and Yesterday

Jane Addams fought for women's rights, peace, and many other ideas. Which idea do you think is most important today? Explain.

Group Activity

Hull House provides many services today. Use the Internet to learn more about them. Then talk in your group about Hull House. Who uses these services? Is Hull House still an important part of the community?

Class Discussion

1. Jane Addams worked for reform her whole life. What kind of person works so hard for reform?

2. Addams spoke out for peace during World War I. Many Americans thought that she was not loyal. Why would people say this? Do you think that Addams was right to speak out? Why or why not?

Reflections

1. Can you use anything from Jane Addams's story in your own life? Explain.

2. How can you learn more about Jane Addams?

Once, someone called Addams "the first citizen of America, the first citizen of the world." Addams answered, "I'm sorry, but [you] . . . must have meant someone else." [3]

What does this tell you about Jane Addams?

Jim Thorpe

"He was the greatest athlete who ever lived."

—Abel Kiviat, 1912 Olympic silver medalist[1]

Pre-Reading Question

What do you know about the Olympic Games?

Reading Preview

Jim Thorpe was one of the world's greatest athletes. He starred in football and track. He won gold medals in two of the hardest events in the Olympics.

Jim Thorpe

Jim Thorpe was an American Indian. He became one of the greatest U.S. athletes.

Beginning on a Reservation

Jim Thorpe was born in Oklahoma in 1888. His ancestors were American Indian and European. His family lived on a reservation. They raised him as an Indian.

At first, Thorpe went to a school on the reservation. But in 1903, his parents sent him to Carlisle Indian School. It was in Pennsylvania.

Football Star

Carlisle was a small school. It had just 250 students. Thorpe joined the football team. By 1908, he was a star. He was named an All-American. That was a great honor, especially for an American Indian from a tiny school.

Thorpe competed in track, too. He ran races, threw the javelin, and made long jumps. These events were new to Thorpe. But he was a natural athlete. And he set records.

$25 a Week

Thorpe left Carlisle in 1909. He played for some professional baseball teams. Thorpe earned about $25 a week. That is about the same as $500 a week now.

In 1911, Thorpe went back to Carlisle. He played football again. Soon, little Carlisle was beating much larger schools. They beat the University of Pittsburgh, and Penn State. They beat Harvard and Princeton.

1912 Olympics

In 1912, Thorpe joined the U.S. Olympic team. The Olympics are held every four years. Athletes from many countries compete.

Thorpe competed in the pentathlon and the decathlon. These are difficult events. The athlete has to run, jump, and throw. Thorpe set records in both events. He got gold medals. People around the world heard about him.

Trouble

After the Olympics, Thorpe went back to Carlisle. He played football again. Then people learned that he played baseball for money. At the time, professional athletes could not compete in the Olympics or in school sports.

Thorpe earned only $25 a week in baseball. It was just enough to live on. And in the Olympics, he competed in track, not baseball. He thought that should be OK.

But the officials didn't agree with him. They took away his records and his gold medals. Thorpe was disappointed. But he couldn't do anything.

Professional Sports

Thorpe decided to play professional sports. He played baseball with the New York Giants and other teams until 1919. But he wasn't a great player.

Then Thorpe turned to football. He played in the National Football League. He was older. But he was still one of the best players.

After Sports

Thorpe quit football in 1929. He was 41 years old. Life became hard for him. He lost his money. He tried to go back into sports, but he was too old. He acted in movies. He even worked for farmers.

In his last years, Thorpe lived in California. He died in 1953. He was 64 years old.

The Greatest Athlete

In 1950, sportswriters chose the greatest athlete from 1900 to 1950. They said that it was Jim Thorpe. In 1963, Thorpe was chosen for the National Football Hall of Fame.

Thorpe's family and friends tried to get his Olympic medals back. At last, the medals were returned to his family in 1982.

Comprehension

Check the answer that completes each sentence correctly.

1. Jim Thorpe grew up

  _____ a. in a large city.

  _____ b. on a reservation.

2. At Carlisle Indian School, Thorpe became

  _____ a. a star football player.

  _____ b. a star basketball player.

3. Thorpe helped Carlisle

  _____ a. beat much larger schools.

  _____ b. start a baseball team.

4. In the 1912 Olympics, Thorpe won gold medals in

  _____ a. baseball.

  _____ b. the pentathlon and the decathlon.

5. Olympic officials took away Thorpe's medals.
   They said that Thorpe was

  _____ a. a professional athlete.

  _____ b. an American Indian.

6. After the Olympics, Thorpe

  _____ a. starred in a movie about his life.

  _____ b. played professional baseball and football.

7. Thorpe's Olympic medals were given back

  _____ a. in the 1940s.

  _____ b. after he was dead.

Sequence

Number the events in the correct order.

_____ Thorpe plays in the National Football League.

_____ Thorpe wins two gold medals in the Olympics.

_____ Sportswriters name Thorpe the greatest athlete.

_____ Thorpe stops playing football.

Vocabulary

Look at these words from the reading. Put a check next to words that you know. Underline words that you don't know yet. Find the words in the reading. Try to guess their meanings.

athlete   natural   record
compete   professional   reservation

Choose the answer that completes each sentence correctly. Write it in the blank.

1. He set _____ at the Olympics. He ran faster than anyone else.
   an athlete/a record

2. Some football players become _____ to make lots of money.
   professional/natural

3. The Thorpe family lived on a _____ in Oklahoma.
   reservation/record

4. Olympic athletes _____ against each other.
   compete/record

5. _____ is someone who plays sports.
   A record/An athlete

6. Thorpe was a _____ athlete. He learned new sports quickly
   reservation/natural

   and easily.

Reading a Chart

Charts show information in rows and columns. This chart lists winners of the decathlon in the Olympic Games from 1912 to 1940.

Olympic Winners in the Decathlon, 1912–1940

Year	Place of Olympics	Decathlon winner	Winner's country
1912	Stockholm, Sweden	Jim Thorpe	United States
1916	Berlin, Germany	Games were not played because of World War I.	
1920	Antwerp, Belgium	Helge Lovland	Norway
1924	Paris, France	Harold Osborn	United States
1928	Amsterdam, Netherlands	Paavo Yrjola	Finland
1932	Los Angeles, U.S.A.	James Bausch	United States
1936	Berlin, Germany	Glenn Morris	United States
1940	Tokyo, Japan	Games were not played because of World War II.	

Read each statement. If it is correct, check *Yes*. If not, check *No*.
Use information from the chart.

Yes   No

____ ____ 1. The 1912 Olympics were played in Stockholm, Sweden.

____ ____ 2. The Olympic Games were played in Tokyo, Japan, in 1940.

____ ____ 3. The winner of the 1928 Olympic decathlon was from Amsterdam, Netherlands.

____ ____ 4. The 1936 Olympic decathlon was won by Glenn Morris.

____ ____ 5. The United States won the Olympic decathlon four times between 1912 and 1940.

Oren Lyons is a chief of the Onondaga nation. He said, "Jim Thorpe was beaten, but he was never tamed . . . . He suffered, but he survived."[2]

Is this a good description of Thorpe's life? Why or why not?

Connecting Today and Yesterday

Are Jim Thorpe's successes important today?
Why or why not?

Group Activity

Professional athletes now complete in some Olympic sports. Think about the following people:

- Jim Thorpe
- Olympic officials in 1912
- Olympic officials today

What would they say about professionals in the Olympics? Role-play a conversation in your group.

Class Discussion

1. How do you think Thorpe felt about losing his Olympic medals?

2. Is it important that Thorpe's medals were returned?

Reflections

1. What is the most interesting thing that you read in this lesson?

2. How can you learn more about Jim Thorpe?

Amelia Earhart

*"As soon as I left the ground,
I knew I myself had to fly."*

—Amelia Earhart, describing
her first ride in an airplane[1]

Pre-Reading Questions

Have you ever wanted to fly a plane? Why or why not?

Reading Preview

Amelia Earhart flew airplanes in the early days of flight.
She set many records. She helped make flying popular.
And she is at the center of one of the great mysteries of the
20th century.

Amelia Earhart

Amelia Earhart was a famous airplane pilot. She set many flying records.

The First Airplane

Amelia Earhart saw her first airplane when she was 10 years old. She didn't think much of it. But at age 20, she took a ride in a small plane. That flight changed her mind. Flying became her main goal in life.

These were the early days of flying. Airplanes were small and primitive. People didn't know much about them. But Earhart made flying popular. She helped make flying part of modern life.

Looking for Adventure

Earhart was born in 1897 in Atchison, Kansas. She always loved adventure. After visiting the St. Louis World's Fair in 1904, she and her sister built a roller coaster. Amelia crashed right away. She said that it was like flying. Their mother made them tear it down.

Earhart loved riding horses. One of her favorite toys was a football. She and her sister had sleds, too. They weren't tiny, safe girls' sleds, either. They were long, fast boys' sleds. Earhart played hard and took chances.

Getting Started

In 1918, many nations were fighting World War I. Earhart wanted to help. She went to Canada and worked in a hospital. She helped care for wounded soldiers.

After the war, Earhart moved to California. Her parents lived there then. That was where she learned to fly.

Her First Flying Record

Earhart took flying lessons in January 1921. Six months later, she bought her first plane. She named it *Canary*, because it was yellow. She set her first flying record in October 1922. She flew *Canary* to an altitude of 14,000 feet. That was a record for women.

Flight across the Atlantic

In 1928, Earhart was asked to fly across the Atlantic Ocean. She flew with two men. She was the first woman to cross the Atlantic in an airplane. People everywhere read about it. Earhart was famous.

Solo Flight

Charles Lindbergh was the first man to fly solo across the Atlantic. He made his famous flight in 1927. Earhart wanted to be the first woman to fly solo across the ocean.

Earhart crossed the Atlantic alone in 1932. The flight was dangerous. She flew through high winds and icy weather. She had problems with her plane. She hoped to land in Paris. Instead, she landed in a field in Ireland.

But the flight was a success. Earhart was more famous than ever. Congress gave her the Distinguished Flying Cross. It was the first time a woman won the award.

Earhart kept flying. She set more records. Some were records for both men and women.

Around the World

In 1937, Earhart wanted another great adventure. She wanted to be the first woman to fly around the world. The distance was 29,000 miles. This time, she flew with Fred Noonan. His job was to read maps and find the way.

Earhart left Oakland, California, on May 21, 1937. They flew east and stopped along the way. They landed at Lae, New Guinea, on June 29.

Howland Island

The next part of the flight was the most dangerous. They would fly 2,556 miles. Then they would try to find Howland Island. It is in the middle of the Pacific Ocean.

Earhart and Noonan left Lae on July 2. It was a cloudy day. The clouds made it hard for Noonan to find the direction. Their radio didn't work well either. They couldn't call for help.

Did you know?

Because Earhart was famous, people paid attention to her clothes. She created Amelia Earhart clothes. They were sold in fancy stores. She said they were "for the woman who lives actively."

Lost in Flight

Earhart and Noonan never reached Howland Island. Did they get lost? Did they run out of fuel? Did they crash in the ocean or on an island? Many people searched for them. But nothing was found. The end of their flight is still a mystery.

Amelia Earhart was lost, but she is remembered. There are many books about her. People talk about the mystery. And they talk about the courage of this early pilot.

Comprehension

Read each statement. If it is correct, check *Yes*. If not, check *No*.

Yes   No

_____ _____ 1. Even as a small child, Earhart wanted to be a pilot.

_____ _____ 2. Earhart flew a plane during World War I.

_____ _____ 3. Earhart set a record in the first plane that she owned.

_____ _____ 4. On her solo flight to Europe, Earhart landed in Ireland.

_____ _____ 5. Earhart was the first person to fly solo across the Atlantic.

_____ _____ 6. Earhart tried to fly around the world by herself.

_____ _____ 7. On her last flight, Earhart's plane was lost in the Pacific. No one knows what happened.

Making Inferences

Read each statement or question. What do you think that Amelia
Earhart would say? Check your answer.

1. Women can't compete with men.

    _____ a. I disagree. There are no limits to what women can do.

    _____ b. I agree. Women don't have the same abilities as men.

2. Should people still try to set flying records?

    _____ a. Yes. By setting records, we learn more about flying.

    _____ b. No. Flying records have no meaning anymore.

3. Should people take chances?

    _____ a. Yes. You must take chances when you try new things.

    _____ b. No. Safety should be your only guide.

Vocabulary

Look at these words from the reading. Put a check next to words that
you know. Underline words that you don't know yet. Find the words
in the reading. Try to guess their meanings.

adventure	mystery	primitive
altitude	pilot	solo

Fill in each blank. Use words from the box.

1. Earhart did everything herself on _____ flights.

2. A professional _____ is paid to fly airplanes.

3. What happened to Amelia Earhart? The answer is a _____.

4. Early planes were made of wood and cloth. They were _____.

5. She flew to an _____ of 14,000 feet—almost 2½ miles above

    the ground.

6. Her first flight was a great _____.

Reading a Map

Physical maps show features of land and water. **Political maps** show the borders of countries, states, and other areas. This map is both a physical and a political map. It shows Earhart's route around the world.

Amelia Earhart's Last Flight

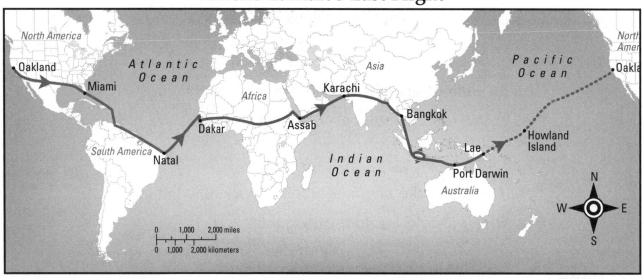

Read each statement. If it is correct, check *Yes*. If not, check *No*.
Use information from the map.

Yes　**No**

_____ _____ 1. Earhart started her flight in Miami.

_____ _____ 2. After Port Darwin, Earhart's next stop was Lae.

_____ _____ 3. The first ocean Earhart crossed was the Pacific.

_____ _____ 4. Earhart flew west around the world.

_____ _____ 5. Earhart flew over five continents.

Connecting Today and Yesterday

In Earhart's time, airplanes were new. It was exciting to be a pilot. There were many records to set. Today, flying is common. What do you think Earhart would do today? Would she still set records? Would she still fly?

Group Activity

Learn more about Earhart's last flight. What risks did she take? What happened to her? Why didn't anyone find her? In your group, talk about what you learn.

Class Discussion

1. What do you think about Earhart's records? Were they worth the risk?

2. Most pilots in the 1920s and 1930s were men. Earhart did many new things for women. Do you think that she made it easier or harder for other women to do new things?

Reflections

1. Can you use anything from Amelia Earhart's story in your own life? Explain.

2. How can you learn more about Amelia Earhart?

Earhart explained why she made dangerous flights. She wrote, "Women must try to do things as men have tried. When they fail, their failure must be but a challenge to others."[2]

What do you think of her reason?

Franz Boas

The Father of American Anthropology

Pre-Reading Questions

Is it important to learn about different cultures? Why or why not?

Reading Preview

Franz Boas was an anthropologist. He studied human culture. He helped people figure out why people behave as they do. He helped us understand ourselves better.

Franz Boas

Franz Boas was an important anthropologist. He helped change the way that people think about culture and race.

Father of American Anthropology

Anthropology is the study of culture and human behavior. It is also the study of where humans came from. Franz Boas is sometimes called the father of American anthropology. He helped begin the study of this science in the United States.

Germany

Boas was born in Minden, Germany, in 1858. He wasn't very healthy as a child. So he spent much of his time reading. He was an intelligent child. And he liked science.

In college, Boas became interested in anthropology. He decided to study it. He got his Ph.D. in 1881.

In 1883, Boas went to Baffin Island in Canada. He studied the culture of native people called the Inuit (pronounced IN-oo-wit). Sometimes these people are called Eskimos, but they prefer the name *Inuit*. And in 1886, Boas went to the Pacific Northwest of North America. There, he studied the culture of the Kwakiutl (pronounced kwah-kee-OO-tul). They are a group of American Indians.

The Kwakiutl

Boas made many later trips to study American Indians, especially the Kwakiutl. He recorded many details about their culture. Modern U.S. culture has changed many Indian cultures. Boas recorded what the Indian cultures were like before they changed.

Boas also studied the languages of the Kwakiutl and other American Indians. He learned that language changes because of culture. But language can also change culture. This was a new way of thinking about both language and culture.

Did you know?

Franz Boas made 13 trips to study native people in the Pacific Northwest. Altogether, he spent 871 days on these trips—nearly 2½ years. He published more than 10,000 pages of information about these cultures.

Becoming an American

After his first visit to the Kwakiutl, Boas decided to stay in the United States. He was a Jew. At that time in Germany, Jews were not treated as equals. So Boas did not return to Germany. He had a better chance to succeed in the United States. He became a U.S. citizen a few years later.

Columbia University

In 1896, Boas began teaching at Columbia University in New York City. Three years later, he became a professor. He was the first professor of anthropology there. He held that job for 37 years. Boas started the first Ph.D. program in anthropology at Columbia.

Ideas about Race and Culture

In the late 1800s, many anthropologists believed that different races of people had different abilities. They said that some races were better than others. And they said that the better races had better cultures.

Boas said that this view was wrong. He argued that culture results from many things. It is affected by what happens to a group of people. Where the group lives also affects their culture. Boas said that race does not control culture.

Changing How People Think

Boas was an important anthropologist. And he did careful work. He had facts and proof to support what he said. He changed the way that anthropologists thought about culture. He also changed how they thought about race.

Today, most people believe that different races are equal. Boas helped convince people of this view. His studies found facts to support it.

Boas's Ideas Living On

Franz Boas died in 1942. But his ideas didn't end. During his life, he taught many students. Some of them became leading anthropologists in the United States. They used his ideas. And they taught new students. So Boas's ideas remain important many years after his death.

Comprehension

Check the answer that completes each sentence correctly.

1. Franz Boas was born in

_____ a. the United States.

_____ b. Germany.

2. Mainly, Boas studied American Indians

_____ a. who lived on Baffin Island.

_____ b. who lived in the Pacific Northwest.

3. The Kwakiutl were

_____ a. American Indians of the Pacific Northwest.

_____ b. a group of Inuit living on Baffin Island.

4. Boas stayed in the United States because

_____ a. he got a job at Columbia University.

_____ b. Jews were treated unfairly in Germany.

5. Boas started the first Ph.D. program in anthropology

_____ a. at Columbia University.

_____ b. in Germany.

6. Boas believed that different races

_____ a. have different abilities.

_____ b. are equal.

7. Boas's ideas are still important. One reason is because

_____ a. he taught students who passed on his ideas.

_____ b. no one else studied the American Indians.

Sequence

Number the events in the correct order.

_____ Boas begins teaching at Columbia University.

_____ Boas begins to study the Kwakiutl.

_____ Boas gets his Ph.D.

_____ Boas studies the Inuit of Baffin Island.

_____ Boas decides to stay in the United States.

Vocabulary

Look at these words from the reading. Put a check next to words that you know. Underline words that you don't know yet. Find the words in the reading. Try to guess their meanings.

anthropology   native   race
equal   professor   science

Choose the answer that completes each sentence correctly. Write it in the blank.

1. In _____, you find facts to explain how things happen.
   professor/science

2. Your success in life should not depend on your _____.
   anthropology/race

3. Many Americans believe that everyone is _____.
   equal/native

4. Boas studied _____ in college.
   anthropology/professor

5. The _____ taught a class about the Kwakiutl.
   professor/science

6. The Kwakiutl lived in America for thousands of years. They are

   _____ people.
   equal/native

Reading a Map

Political maps show the borders of countries, states, and other areas. **Physical maps** show features of land and water. This map is both a political and a physical map. It shows some of the American Indian groups that lived in the Pacific Northwest. Boas studied these groups.

Some American Indians of the Pacific Northwest

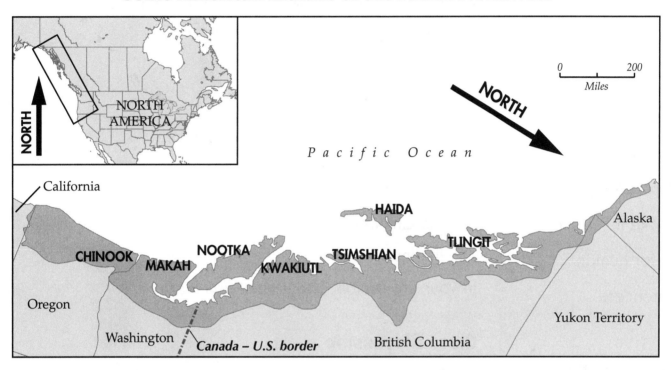

Choose the answer that completes each sentence correctly. Write it in the blank. Use information from the map.

1. The Makah live mainly in _____.

Washington/Oregon

2. The Tsimshian live north of _____.

the Kwakiutl/the Tlingit

3. The Haida live on an island in _____.

the Pacific/Oregon

4. The Kwakiutl live mainly in _____.

the U.S./Canada

5. The Chinook live in an area that is about _____ from north to south.

1,800 miles/300 miles

Connecting Today and Yesterday

Do you think that anthropology is important today? Why or why not?

Group Activity

Learn about one of these groups of native people:

- the Tlingit
- the Haida
- the Tsimshian
- the Kwakiutl
- the Nootka
- the Makah
- the Chinook
- the Inuit

In your group, talk about what you learn.

Class Discussion

1. Why do you think Boas traveled far to study small groups of people? Was there something to learn from these people? Could he have learned the same things by studying culture in New York? Explain.

2. Does anthropology interest you? Why or why not?

Reflections

1. What was the most interesting thing that you read in this lesson?

2. How can you learn more about Franz Boas?

Ruth Benedict, a famous anthropologist, was one of Boas's students. She said, "The purpose of anthropology is to make the world safe for human differences."[1]

Do you think that Boas would agree with her? Do you agree with her? Why or why not?

Louis Armstrong

"What a wonderful world it would be if only we would give it a chance. Love, baby, love. That's the secret."

—Louis Armstrong[1]

Pre-Reading Questions

What do you know about jazz? Do you like it? Explain.

Reading Preview

Louis Armstrong was one of the greatest jazz musicians. He helped make jazz popular. People from many countries came to hear him play and sing.

Louis Armstrong

Louis Armstrong helped create jazz. He became one of the greatest jazz musicians.

A Tough Beginning

Louis Armstrong was born on August 4, 1901, in New Orleans. His early life was hard. He grew up in a tough part of the city. His father left the family when Armstrong was a baby. They were poor. When he was very young, Armstrong began working. He helped neighbors. He collected junk to sell. He sang on the streets for tips.

His First Music Lessons

When he was 11, Armstrong fired a gun on New Year's Eve. The police came. A judge put Armstrong in a children's home. There, he had his first music lessons. He played a cornet, a kind of horn, in the school band.

After Armstrong left the children's home, he earned his living as a musician. He performed with top musicians in New Orleans. One of the best was Joe Oliver. Oliver was almost like a father to Armstrong. He taught Armstrong a lot about playing the cornet.

A New Kind of Music

Armstrong performed jazz. This was a special New Orleans style of music. It was partly blues and partly ragtime. Armstrong was one of the first to play it.

Jazz musicians like Armstrong didn't just play music as it was written. They might start with a popular song. Then they would add to it and change it. They turned it into art.

Moving North

By 1922, Armstrong was one of the top musicians in New Orleans. He sang and played the cornet. But he was black. And most black musicians had to play at cheap bars. By then, Joe Oliver was in Chicago. He asked Armstrong to join him. Armstrong would have more chances there. So Armstrong moved to Chicago too.

New York

Two years later, Armstrong was invited to New York City. He played the trumpet in New York. Later, the trumpet became his main instrument.

Armstrong's music was unusual. He had a different style and great skill. Some people didn't know what to think about his music. Others loved it.

Recording His Music

In 1925, Armstrong went back to Chicago. He began recording his music. He made some of the most famous recordings in jazz history. They included the songs "Cornet Chop," "Heebie Jeebies," and "Hotter Than That."

Changing Music

Armstrong's music was different from other musicians' music. He used the cornet and trumpet as solo instruments. Other bands used several instruments at once.

Armstrong also sang scat. Scat is a special kind of jazz singing. The singer uses made-up words that don't mean anything. Armstrong used scat singing to make his music even more creative. Armstrong didn't invent scat. But he made it popular.

Other musicians listened to Armstrong's music. They tried to do some of the same things. Armstrong was changing American music. He changed the way jazz was played. He changed other kinds of music, too.

World-Famous

In the 1930s and most of the 1940s, Armstrong played with a large band. He played a type of jazz called "swing." His band was one of the most popular groups in the United States.

In the late 1940s, people got tired of swing. So Armstrong changed his style. He also formed a smaller band. It was called the Louis Armstrong All-Stars. The band traveled to Europe, South America, Africa, Asia, and across the United States. In 1956, he gave a concert in Ghana, Africa. More than 100,000 people came.

Did you know?

Armstrong was sometimes called "Satchmo." He got the name because he had a large mouth. People called him "Satchelmouth." A satchel is a large bag or suitcase. "Satchmo" was short for "Satchelmouth."

Armstrong gave about 300 concerts each year. And he made thousands of recordings. Many are still in stores.

The Last Years

Armstrong was not healthy during his last years. But he kept working. He died in 1971. Newspapers around the world reported his death. His coffin was in New York City. More than 25,000 people came to say good-bye.

Comprehension

Read each statement. If it is correct, check *Yes*. If not, check *No*.

Yes   No

_____ _____ 1. Armstrong grew up in a tough New York neighborhood.

_____ _____ 2. The first instrument that Armstrong played was a trumpet.

_____ _____ 3. Armstrong was one of the earliest jazz musicians.

_____ _____ 4. The Louis Armstrong All-Stars played swing music.

_____ _____ 5. Armstrong invented scat singing.

_____ _____ 6. Armstrong played jazz, but his work changed other kinds of music too.

_____ _____ 7. Armstrong made thousands of recordings.

Cause and Effect

Read each statement. What was the result? Check the result.

1. Armstrong shot a gun on New Year's Eve. As a result,

    _____ a. he was sent to a children's home.

    _____ b. he was invited to join a band in New York.

2. In New Orleans, Armstrong could play only in cheap bars. As a result,

    _____ a. he started playing with Joe Oliver.

    _____ b. he moved to Chicago.

3. Armstrong began to sing scat. As a result,

    _____ a. he gave a concert in Ghana, Africa.

    _____ b. scat became popular.

4. People got tired of swing music. As a result,

    _____ a. Armstrong changed his style of playing.

    _____ b. Armstrong went to Europe and Africa to play.

Vocabulary

Look at these words from the reading. Put a check next to words that you know. Underline words that you don't know yet. Find the words in the reading. Try to guess their meanings.

concert   musician   recordings
instrument   perform

Fill in each blank. Use words from the box.

1. More than 100,000 people came to the _____.

2. Many people bought Armstrong's _____.

3. Armstrong liked to _____ before a large audience.

4. Armstrong's favorite _____ was the trumpet.

5. The _____ played the piano and the drums.

Reading a Time Line

Time lines show events in order on a line. This time line shows events in Louis Armstrong's life.

The Life of Louis Armstrong

1922
Armstrong moves to Chicago; joins Joe Oliver's Creole Jazz Band.

1947
Armstrong plays at Carnegie Hall in New York City.

1901
Louis Armstrong is born in New Orleans.

1925
Armstrong makes his first recording with his own band.

1964
Armstrong records "Hello Dolly," which becomes the best-selling recording in the U.S.

| 1900 | 1910 | 1920 | 1930 | 1940 | 1950 | 1960 | 1970 | 1980 |

1912
Armstrong is placed in a children's home.

1936
Armstrong acts in the movie *Pennies from Heaven*.

1971
Armstrong dies in New York City.

1924
Armstrong moves to New York City.

1948
Armstrong performs in Nice, France, at the first international jazz festival.

Fill in each blank. Use information from the time line.

1. Armstrong was placed in a children's home in the year _____.

2. Armstrong was _____ years old when he moved to New York City.

3. Armstrong played in the Nice International Jazz Festival _____ years after he made his first recording with his own band.

4. Armstrong recorded "Hello Dolly" _____ years after he played at Carnegie Hall.

5. Armstrong acted in *Pennies from Heaven* in the year _____.

Connecting Today and Yesterday

Louis Armstrong was one of the greatest jazz musicians. Is his work important today? Why or why not?

Group Activity

Get some of Louis Armstrong's recordings from the library. In your group, listen to music from different times in his life. Talk about the music. Discuss these questions:

- What do you like about it?
- How does it make you feel?
- Do you like his early recordings or his later ones better? Why?
- How is this music different from what you usually listen to?

Class Discussion

1. How do you think music changed Louis Armstrong's life? Explain.

2. Armstrong performed his music around the world. Many people came to hear him. Why do you think he was so popular in other countries? Do you think that Armstrong's performances changed how people thought of the United States? Explain.

Reflections

1. Can you use anything from Louis Armstrong's story in your own life? Explain.

2. How can you learn more about Louis Armstrong?

Louis Armstrong said, "I never tried to prove nothing, just wanted to give a good show . . . . The main thing is to live for that audience, 'cause what you're there for is to please the people." [2]

How does this statement make you feel about Armstrong?

John Glenn

"There are times when you [give] yourself to a higher cause than personal safety."

—*John Glenn*[1]

Pre-Reading Question

What do you know about the first U.S. missions into space?

Reading Preview

John Glenn was the first U.S. astronaut to fly around the earth in a space capsule. And he went into space again 36 years later. He was the oldest person ever to go into space.

John Glenn

John Glenn was one of the first U.S. astronauts. He was the first American to orbit the earth in a spaceship.

Early Life

John Glenn was born in 1921 in Cambridge, Ohio. He grew up in nearby New Concord. There he met Annie Castor. She was a neighbor and the daughter of family friends. Later they married and had two children.

In 1941, the United States entered World War II. Glenn joined the Marine Corps. He became a fighter pilot. He flew many dangerous missions. World War II ended in 1945. But in 1950, the Korean War started. Glenn flew fighter planes again.

Test Pilot

After the Korean War, Glenn became a test pilot. It was a dangerous job. He needed courage and special skills.

Glenn was one of the best U.S. test pilots. He set a new speed record. He flew a plane from Los Angeles to New York in 3 hours and 23 minutes.

Into Space

In the 1950s, the United States and the Soviet Union were enemies. Both had strong armies and awful weapons. They were the world's most powerful countries.

Then in 1957, the Soviet Union sent a rocket into space. It carried a satellite that orbited the earth. This event showed that the Soviet Union had a powerful rocket. And it proved that the Soviet Union was ahead of the United States in space science. President Eisenhower said the United States must catch up.

The United States started its own space program in 1958. The program was run by the National Aeronautics and Space Administration, or NASA. It started with seven astronauts in 1959. John Glenn was one of these first astronauts.

First Flight

Glenn went into space in 1962. He was the third U.S. astronaut in space. The two before him had very short missions. They came down without circling the earth.

Glenn went on a longer mission. It lasted almost five hours. He was the first U.S. astronaut to orbit the earth.

Almost a Disaster

The capsule orbited the earth three times. Then it was time to land. Glenn learned that the outside of the capsule was damaged. No one knew how bad the damage was. A space capsule gets very hot flying through the earth's atmosphere. Glen hoped that his capsule would not burn up.

Glenn was busy with his controls. The outside of the capsule glowed. Flames shot by his window. Later, he said that the minutes passed "like days on a calendar."[2]

But the capsule didn't burn up. Glenn landed safely. He became a national hero.

United States Senator

Glenn left NASA in 1964. He quit the Marines a year later. In 1974, he was elected to the U.S. Senate from Ohio. Glenn served there until 1999.

Return to Space

In 1998, Glenn went into space again. He was on the crew of the space shuttle *Discovery*. The mission lasted almost nine days. Glenn was 77 years old. He was the oldest person ever to fly in space. Scientists wanted to learn how spaceflight affects the bodies of older people. The mission was a success. Glenn was a hero again.

After Space and the Senate

John Glenn still works. He writes, and he speaks to groups. He and his wife also work with the John Glenn Institute. The Institute is part of Ohio State University. Glenn's papers are collected there. The Institute supports public service. It helps students be active citizens.

Comprehension

Check the answer that completes each sentence correctly.

1. John Glenn was born in

   _____ a. Ohio.

   _____ b. New York.

2. During World War II, Glenn

   _____ a. joined NASA.

   _____ b. flew fighter planes.

3. The United States started its space program

   _____ a. to keep up with the Soviet Union.

   _____ b. to win World War II.

4. Glenn was the first U.S. astronaut

   _____ a. to go into space.

   _____ b. to orbit the earth.

5. On Glenn's first spaceflight,

   _____ a. he set a speed record.

   _____ b. his capsule was damaged.

6. After Glenn left NASA,

   _____ a. he became a senator.

   _____ b. he became a test pilot.

7. Glenn went back into space in 1998

   _____ a. and orbited the earth for the first time.

   _____ b. when he was 77 years old.

Making Inferences

Read the statement. What do you think that John Glenn would say? Check your answer.

1. War is a terrible waste of human life.

    _____ a. Yes. Our country should never go to war.

    _____ b. Yes, but sometimes people have to fight.

2. The United States should send astronauts to other planets.

    _____ a. No. Exploring space is a waste of money.

    _____ b. Yes. Humans must never stop exploring.

3. Older people should not push themselves too hard.

    _____ a. I disagree. Older people can do more than you think.

    _____ b. I agree. Older people have done enough.

Vocabulary

Look at these words from the reading. Put a check next to words that you know. Underline words that you don't know yet. Find the words in the reading. Try to guess their meanings.

astronaut	mission	satellite
atmosphere	orbit	space capsules

Fill in each blank. Use words from the box.

1. The earliest _____ had room for just one person.

2. Glenn was the first U.S. astronaut to _____ the earth.

3. An _____ wears a special suit in space.

4. A _____ orbits the earth.

5. John Glenn went on a _____ to explore space.

6. The air is called the earth's _____.

Reading a Chart

Charts show information in rows and columns. This chart lists some important U.S. spaceflights.

Some Major U.S. Spaceflights

Name of capsule	Date	Astronauts	What happened
Freedom 7	1961	Alan Shepard	Shepard was the first U.S. astronaut in space.
Friendship 7	1962	John Glenn	Glenn was the first U.S. astronaut to orbit the earth.
Faith 7	1963	Gordon Cooper	This was the U.S.'s final and longest one-man mission. It lasted 34 hours.
Gemini 4	1965	James McDivitt Edward White	White was the first U.S. astronaut to walk in space.
Apollo 8	1968	Frank Borman Jim Lovell William Anders	This was the first mission to reach and orbit the moon.
Apollo 11	1969	Neil Armstrong Michael Collins Edwin Aldrin	This was the first mission to land on the moon. Armstrong was the first man to walk on the moon.

Fill in each blank. Use information from the chart.

1. _____ was the first astronaut to walk in space.

2. Borman, Lovell, and Anders flew in a capsule named _____.

3. Neil Armstrong walked on the moon in the year _____.

4. The first U.S. astronaut to go into space was _____.

5. The longest U.S. one-man mission lasted _____.

John Glenn talked about the day that he orbited the earth. He said, "What can you say about a day in which you get to see four sunsets?"[3]

How did Glenn see four sunsets? What did he mean?

Connecting Today and Yesterday

The U.S. space program was started to keep up with the Soviet Union. The United States does not have to keep up now. Do you think that the United States should still explore space? Explain.

Group Activity

The early U.S. space missions were divided into three programs: the Mercury program, the Gemini program, and the Apollo program. Learn about one of these programs. In your group, talk about what you learn.

Class Discussion

1. Why do you think John Glenn did so many dangerous jobs?
2. John Glenn had many important jobs. Which do you think was most important? Explain.

Reflections

1. What is the most interesting thing that you read in this lesson?
2. How can you learn more about John Glenn?

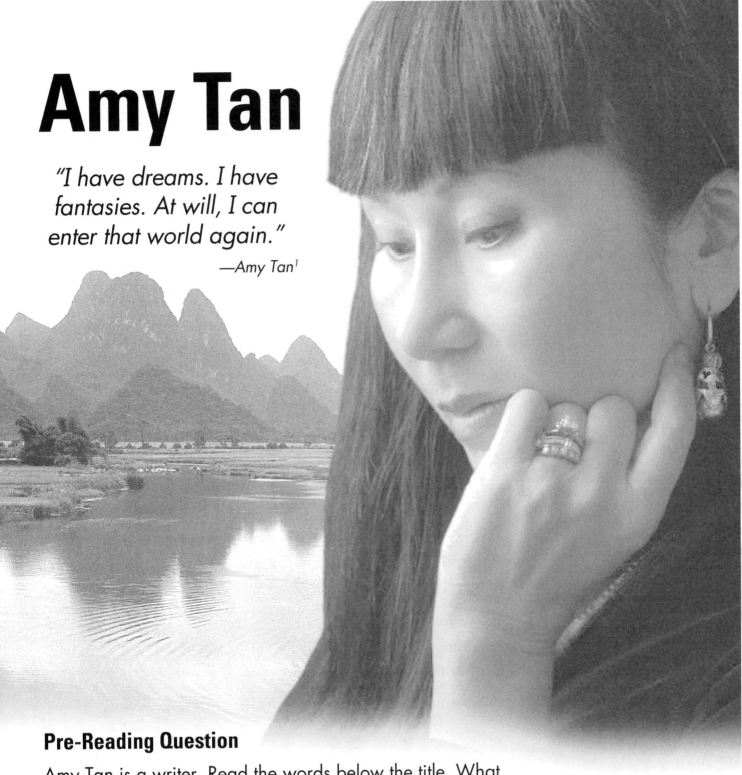

Amy Tan

"I have dreams. I have fantasies. At will, I can enter that world again."

—Amy Tan[1]

Pre-Reading Question

Amy Tan is a writer. Read the words below the title. What do you think that they mean?

Reading Preview

Amy Tan is an important U.S. writer. She writes fiction as well as nonfiction. She writes about mothers and daughters. And she writes about life as both a Chinese and an American woman.

Amy Tan

Amy Tan writes books that are read by millions of people. They show how people of different cultures and ages are alike and different.

A Chinese and American Childhood

Amy Tan's father came to the United States from China in 1947. Her mother came here in 1949. Tan was born in Oakland, California, in 1952. Her parents named her En-Mai. The name means "Blessing of America."

Tan learned Chinese and English as a child. And she learned both Chinese and U.S. culture.

Family Tragedies

Tan's older brother, Peter, died of brain cancer in 1967. Her father died of cancer a few months later. After these tragedies, Tan's mother moved to Europe with Amy and her younger brother, John. They lived first in the Netherlands and then in Switzerland.

Tan was angry over the tragedies. She rebelled and got into trouble. She made new friends who used drugs. She was even arrested. But she learned from her mistakes.

Back to the United States

Tan finished high school in Switzerland. Then Tan's mother brought the family back to the United States.

Tan started college in Oregon. She planned to become a doctor. Then she changed her mind. She studied English.

At about this time, Tan met Louis DiMattei. They fell in love. So she went to San Jose State University. There, she could be with Lou. They were married in 1974.

Tragedy Again

Tan's life seemed good. But then tragedy came again. Her best friend was murdered. Tan's anger and feeling of loss returned.

Because of this loss, Tan quit school and began working. She had several jobs. Then she started a business. She worked long hours as a business writer. In fact, she worked too many hours. She had to make a change. So she began learning jazz piano and writing fiction.

The Joy Luck Club

Tan first wrote short stories. One of them, "Rules of the Game," was published in 1987. She wrote more stories. She turned them into her first novel, *The Joy Luck Club*. It was published in 1989.

The Joy Luck Club tells about a young Chinese-American woman. Her Chinese mother died recently. So the woman visits her mother's Chinese friends. The novel shows that people are different because of age and culture. But they are also alike. *The Joy Luck Club* became a best-seller in the United States.

Other Books

Tan wrote a second novel. She called it *The Kitchen God's Wife*. It is also about a young woman and her Chinese mother. This book shows how the two women do not understand each other. They love each other. But they are sometimes angry with each other. Many people admire *The Kitchen God's Wife*.

Tan's next novels were *The Hundred Secret Senses* and *The Bonesetter's Daughter*. These books also look at mothers and daughters.

In 2003, Tan wrote *The Opposite of Fate: A Book of Musings*. It is not fiction. It tells about her life and what she thinks.

Her Mother's Stories

Tan began writing to understand herself. Her writing also helped her learn about her Chinese culture. And it helped her understand her mother. Her books, she said, include her mother's stories.

Did you know?

In 1991, Amy Tan joined a rock 'n' roll band—The Rock Bottom Remainders. The band is made up of writers. Together, they've published more than 150 books. Stephen King, Scott Turow, and Dave Barry are also in the band.

"My books," she said, "have amounted to taking her stories—a gift to me—and giving them back to her. To me, it was the [best] thing I ever could have done for myself and my mother."[2]

Many people feel that Tan's books are also gifts to them. These gifts help them see how people of every culture are alike. And they are gifts that tell how different cultures make the United States richer and more interesting.

Comprehension

Read each statement. If it is correct, check *Yes*. If not, check *No*.

Yes   **No**

_____ _____   1. Tan was born in Switzerland.

_____ _____   2. Tan learned Chinese and English as a child.

_____ _____   3. Tan's mother was an American. Her father was Chinese.

_____ _____   4. Tan's father and brother died at about the same time.

_____ _____   5. Tragedy caused major changes in Tan's life.

_____ _____   6. *The Opposite of Fate: A Book of Musings* was Tan's first book.

_____ _____   7. Tan writes about her Chinese culture.

Cause and Effect

Read each statement. What was the result? Check the result.

1. Tan's brother Peter died of brain cancer. As a result,

   _____ a. Tan's father died of brain cancer.

   _____ b. Tan became angry.

2. Tan rebelled and got into trouble. As a result,

   _____ a. she finished high school.

   _____ b. she was arrested.

3. Tan's best friend was murdered. As a result,

   _____ a. Tan quit school and got a job.

   _____ b. Tan moved to Europe with her family.

4. Tan began writing fiction. As a result,

   _____ a. she learned about herself and her mother.

   _____ b. she stopped writing short stories.

Vocabulary

Look at these words from the reading. Put a check next to words that you know. Underline words that you don't know yet. Find the words in the reading. Try to guess their meanings.

fiction   rebelled   tragedy

novel   short story

Fill in each blank. Use words from the box.

1. A novel is longer than a _____.

2. Tan's best friend was murdered. It was a _____.

3. It was a long _____. But I read the book in a week.

4. Tan got in trouble when she _____.

5. Novels and short stories are both _____.

Reading a Time Line

Time lines show events in order on a line. This time line shows events in Amy Tan's life.

The Life of Amy Tan

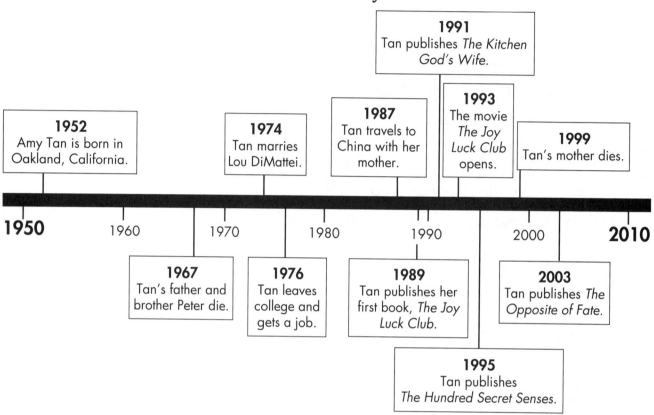

Read each statement. If it is correct, check *Yes*. If not, check *No*.
Use information from the time line.

Yes   **No**

____ ____ 1. Tan's mother died in 1999.

____ ____ 2. Tan was about 32 years old when she married.

____ ____ 3. Tan was about 37 years old when she published *The Joy Luck Club*.

____ ____ 4. *The Kitchen God's Wife* was published after *The Hundred Secret Senses*.

____ ____ 5. The movie *The Joy Luck Club* opened in 1993.

Connecting Today and Yesterday

Amy Tan writes about mothers and daughters. She also writes about U.S. and Chinese culture. Are these important ideas to talk about in the United States today? Explain.

Group Activity

In your group, watch the movie *The Joy Luck Club.* Then talk about it.

Class Discussion

1. Would you like to meet Amy Tan? Why or why not? What questions would you ask her?

2. The United States has many cultures. Do you think that these cultures make the country richer and more interesting? Why or why not?

Reflections

1. Can you use anything from Amy Tan's story in your own life? Explain.

2. How can you learn more about Amy Tan?

Amy Tan said, "The best stories do change us. They help us live interesting lives." [3]

What do you think Tan meant? Do you agree with her?

Jaime Escalante

"Many people think computers are going to do everything for you. They don't realize . . . the best computer is your brain."

—Jaime Escalante[1]

Pre-Reading Questions

Who were your best teachers? What made them good?

Reading Preview

Jaime Escalante was one of the best teachers in the United States. He found ways to make students want to learn. And he helped them succeed. He became known across the country.

Jaime Escalante

Jaime Escalante is a great teacher. He motivates his students to learn and succeed.

Born in Bolivia

Jaime Escalante's parents lived in Bolivia. Escalante was born there. His parents broke up when he was 9. His mother took the children to the city of La Paz.

Teacher

Both of Escalante's parents were teachers. And one of his grandparents was a teacher. In 1952, he became a teacher too. He taught mathematics in Bolivia until 1963.

In 1964, Escalante came to the United States. He wanted to teach here, too. But he didn't have a teaching certificate. And he couldn't speak English. So Escalante went to college. In 1972, he earned a degree in mathematics. In 1974, he got his teaching certificate.

Garfield High School

Escalante started teaching at Garfield High School in 1976. It is in East Los Angeles. Most of his students were from low-income Hispanic neighborhoods. These were tough neighborhoods. Drugs, gangs, and violence were common. No one expected much from these students.

But Escalante was a great teacher. He taught a special class in calculus. He used activities and games to get students interested. He made jokes and scolded them. He used examples that they understood. He challenged them and made them work. He proved to them that they could succeed.

The AP Test

In 1982, Escalante's students took the Advanced Placement (AP) test in calculus. If they passed, it would help them in college. Every student passed. This was unusual. It was especially unusual for students in schools like Garfield.

People from the testing service couldn't believe the results. They asked, "Did the students cheat?"

The students took the test again. This time, the testing service gave the test. And the students passed again. They proved that Escalante was a great teacher. He became famous across the United States.

Ganas

People listened to Escalante speak about education. And each year, he built a stronger mathematics program at Garfield. More and more students passed the AP calculus test.

Escalante says that all students can succeed. A banner in his classroom said, "Ganas." *Ganas* means "desire." Students need *ganas,* says Escalante. A teacher must help students find *ganas.*

Stand and Deliver

In 1988, a movie called *Stand and Deliver* was released. It was about Escalante. It showed how he motivated his students. It showed the students' neighborhoods. It showed how a good teacher can change students' lives.

Futures with Jaime Escalante

In 1990, the Public Broadcasting Service (PBS) did a TV show with Escalante. It was called *Futures with Jaime Escalante.* It told students about jobs in math and science. *Futures* was the most popular classroom show in the history of PBS. It won more than 50 awards.

New Challenges

At age 60, Escalante left Garfield High School. He began teaching in the Sacramento school system. He chose the hardest school in the system. As before, he helped his students succeed.

Escalante retired in 1998. Then he went back to Bolivia. He lived in a small village there. He taught part-time. He died in 2010, at age 79.

Did you know?

In 1999, Jaime Escalante was elected to the National Teachers Hall of Fame. It honors the best teachers in the United States.

Comprehension

Check the answer that completes each sentence correctly.

1. Jaime Escalante was born in

    _____ a. Bolivia.

    _____ b. California.

2. Escalante couldn't teach in the United States because he

    _____ a. didn't know how to teach.

    _____ b. didn't have a teaching certificate.

3. Escalante's students at Garfield were mainly

    _____ a. from low-income Hispanic neighborhoods.

    _____ b. from rich families.

4. When Escalante's students took the AP calculus test, they all

    _____ a. cheated.

    _____ b. passed.

5. Escalante said that all students need

    _____ a. mathematics.

    _____ b. *ganas.*

6. *Stand and Deliver* is

    _____ a. a movie about Escalante.

    _____ b. a book written by Escalante.

7. After Escalante retired, he

    _____ a. made a TV show on PBS.

    _____ b. went back to Bolivia to live.

Making Inferences

Read each statement or question. What do you think that Jaime Escalante would say? Check your answer.

1. All children can succeed in school.

    _____ a. Yes. Poor children can learn as well as rich children.

    _____ b. No. Rich children will usually do better.

2. Teachers can't help students who don't want to learn.

    _____ a. I agree. Some students just don't want to learn.

    _____ b. I disagree. Teachers must find ways to motivate them.

3. Why is teaching a good job?

    _____ a. Teachers are paid well.

    _____ b. Teachers build the future through their students.

4. Why should we study math? Only a few jobs use it.

    _____ a. You should study math only if you like it.

    _____ b. Learning math can help you learn to succeed.

Vocabulary

Look at these words from the reading. Put a check next to words that you know. Underline words that you don't know yet. Find the words in the reading. Try to guess their meanings.

certificate	education	motivate
challenged	mathematics	

Fill in each blank. Use words from the box.

1. The _____ showed that Escalante was trained to teach.

2. Escalante _____ his students and made them work.

3. When you study _____, you learn how to use numbers.

4. You can get a good _____ at many colleges.

5. Escalante wanted to _____ his students.

Reading a Chart

Charts show information in rows and columns. This chart lists information about teachers in the National Teachers Hall of Fame. It tells about the five who were chosen in 1999.

National Teachers Hall of Fame for 1999

Teacher	Subjects Taught	Home	Years Teaching
Jaime Escalante	mathematics	Granite Bay, California	33 years
Dorothy Kittaka	music	Fort Wayne, Indiana	28 years
Debra Peppers	English, speech, debate, theater	St. Louis, Missouri	25 years
Ronald Poplau	sociology and community service	Shawnee Mission, Kansas	36 years
Vicki Roscoe	curriculum resource teacher	Orlando, Florida	20 years

Choose the answer that completes each sentence correctly. Write it in the blank. Use information from the chart.

1. _____ taught the longest.
   Jaime Escalante/Ronald Poplau

2. Dorothy Kittaka taught _____.
   mathematics/music

3. Vicki Roscoe taught for _____.
   20 years/25 years

4. _____ taught English.
   Vicki Roscoe/Debra Peppers

5. Ronald Poplau lived in _____.
   Florida/Kansas

Ann Plato was a teacher in Hartford, Connecticut. In 1841, she said, "A good education is another name for happiness."[2]

What did she mean? Do you agree with her? Why or why not?

Connecting Today and Yesterday

Escalante chose to teach in the toughest neighborhoods. He helped his students succeed. Do you think that Escalante would still succeed in tough schools today? Why or why not?

Group Activity

Think about your best teachers. List your answers to these questions:

- Why did you like them?
- How did they help you learn?
- How did they keep you interested?
- Why were they so good?

Talk about your answers in your group.

Class Discussion

1. Escalante taught mathematics. Do you think that his way of teaching is useful for other subjects? Explain.
2. Escalante used different ways to motivate students. Sometimes he scolded. He made jokes and played games. He challenged students. Are these good ways of teaching? Explain.

Reflections

1. Can you use anything from Jaime Escalante's story in your own life? Explain.
2. How can you learn more about Jaime Escalante?

Notes and References

Abigail Adams

Notes

1. Abigail Adams, quoted in *"First Thoughts": Life and Letters of Abigail Adams*, p. 14.
2. Abigail Adams, Letter from Abigail Adams to John Adams, October 22, 1775, in *Adams Family Papers: An Electronic Archive*. Text at Massachusetts Historical Society, www.masshist.org/digitaladams/aea/cfm/doc.cfm?id=L17751022aa.

References

Gelles, Edith G. *"First Thoughts": Life and Letters of Abigail Adams*. New York: Twayne Publishers, 1998.

Gelles, Edith G. *Portia: The World of Abigail Adams*. Bloomington, IN: Indiana University Press, 1992.

McCullough, David. *John Adams*. New York: Simon & Schuster, 2001.

Nagel, Paul C. *The Adams Women: Abigail and Louisa Adams, Their Sisters and Daughters*. New York: Oxford University Press, 1987.

Osborne, Angela. *Abigail Adams*. New York: Chelsea House Publishers, 1989.

George Washington

Notes

1. King William IV, quoted in *George Washington: A Biography*, p. 304.
2. John Marshall, quoted in "George Washington: Life after the Presidency."
3. Henry Lee, quoted in *Founding Father: Rediscovering George Washington*, p. 199.

References

Alden, John R. *George Washington: A Biography*. Baton Rouge, LA: Louisiana State University Press, 1984.

"The Apotheosis of George Washington: Brumidi's Fresco and Beyond." On the web site of the American Studies program at the University of Virginia, xroads.Virginia.edu/~CAP/gw/gwmain.html.

Brookhiser, Richard. *Founding Father: Rediscovering George Washington*. New York: The Free Press, 1996.

"George Washington." On the web site of the White House, www.whitehouse.gov/history/presidents/gw1.html.

"George Washington: Life after the Presidency." On the web site of the National Park Service, www.cr.nps.gov/logcabin/html/gw5.html.

Randall, Willard Sterne. *George Washington: A Life*. New York: Henry Holt, 1997.

Paul Revere

Notes

1. Obituary for Paul Revere in the *Boston Intelligence*, quoted at theamericanrevolution.org/ipeople/prevere.asp

References

Fischer, David Hackett. *Paul Revere's Ride*. New York: Oxford University Press, 1994.

Garraty, John A., and Mark C. Carnes, gen. ed. *American National Biography*. New York: Oxford University Press, 1999.

"Patriots Day," on the web site of *The American Experience*, www.pbs.org/wgbh/amex/patriotsday/peopleevents/p_revere.html.

"Paul Revere's Account of His Midnight Ride to Lexington." Text on "America's Homepage" by Steven Thomas, ahp.gatech.edu/midnight_ride_1775.html.

Scheer, George F., and Hugh F. Rankin. *Rebels and Redcoats: The Living Story of the American Revolution*. New York: World Publishing, 1957.

Noah Webster

Notes

1. Henry Ward Beecher, quoted on the web site of the University Writing Center, University of Northern Colorado, asweb.unco.edu/depts/english/wcenter/quotes.htm.

References

Garraty, John A., and Mark C. Carnes, gen. ed. *American National Biography*. New York: Oxford University Press, 1999.

Rollins, Richard M. *The Long Journey of Noah Webster*. Philadelphia: University of

Pennsylvania Press, 1980.

"A Short Summary of Noah Webster's Life." On the web site of Connecticut State University, www.ctstateu.edu/noahweb/biography.html.

Ulysses S. Grant

Notes

1. James Longstreet, in an interview for the *New York Times,* July 24, 1885, quoted in *Ulysses S. Grant Association Newsletter*, January 1965. Text online at www.lib.siu.edu/projects/usgrant/newsletter/newsletter.html

2. Abraham Lincoln, quoted in *Ulysses S. Grant: Triumph over Adversity, 1822–1865,* p. 462.

References

"Historical Information on Ulysses S. Grant." On the web site of the Ulysses S. Grant Association, www.lib.siu.edu/projects/usgrant/.

McFeely, William S. *Ulysses S. Grant: An Album.* New York: W.W. Norton, 2004.

Simpson, Brooks D. *Ulysses S. Grant: Triumph over Adversity, 1822–1865,* Boston: Houghton Mifflin, 2000.

"Ulysses S. Grant." On the web site of the White House, www.whitehouse.gov/history/presidents/ug18.html.

"Ulysses S. Grant: Eighteenth President 1869–1877." On the web site of National Park Service, www.cr.nps.gov/logcabin/html/usg.html.

"Ulysses S. Grant," on "Ulysses S. Grant Homepage," by Candace Scott, www.mscomm.com/~ulysses/.

Sojourner Truth

Notes

1. Sojourner Truth as quoted by Harriet Beecher Stowe in "Sojourner Truth, the Libyan Sibyl," quoted in *Glorying in Tribulation: The Lifework of Sojourner Truth,* pp. 87–88.

2. Sojourner Truth at the Women's Rights Convention in Worcester, Massachusetts, October 1850, quoted by Faye Wattleton in "An Open Letter to My Daughter." Text online on the web site of Gifts of Speech at Sweet Briar College, gos.sbc.edu/w/wattleton.html.

References

Historical Census Browser, Geospatial & Statistical Data Center. On the web site of the University of Virginia Library, fisher.lib.virginia.edu/collections/stats/histcensus.

Painter, Nell Irvin. *Sojourner Truth: A Life, a Symbol.* New York: W.W. Norton, 1996.

Stetson, Erlene and Linda David. *Glorying in Tribulation: The Lifework of Sojourner Truth.* East Lansing, Michigan: Michigan State University Press, 1994.

Truth, Sojourner. *Narrative of Sojourner Truth,* edited by Margaret Washington. New York: Vintage Books, 1993.

Thomas Edison

Notes

1. Thomas Edison, quoted in "Edison Invents."

References

"Edison Invents." On the web site of the Lemelson Center, Smithsonian National Museum of American History, invention.smithsonian.org/centerpieces/edison/000_resources_01.asp.

Heyn, Ernest V. *Fire of Genius: Inventors of the Past Century.* Garden City, New York: Anchor Press/Doubleday, 1976.

Davis, L.J. *Fleet Fire: Thomas Edison and the Pioneers of the Electric Revolution.* New York: Arcade Publishing, 2003.

Jones, Jill. *Empires of Light: Edison, Tesla, Westinghouse, and the Race to Electrify the World.* New York: Random House, 2003.

Jane Addams

Notes

1. Jane Addams, quoted in "Hull-House Incorporated," on the web site of the American Studies program at the University of Virginia, xroads.virginia.edu/~HYPER/INCORP/Hull-House/jane.html.

2. "Jane Addams: A Foe of War and Need," *New York Times,* May 22, 1935, on the web site of the *New York Times,* www.nytimes.com/learning/general/onthisday/bday/0906.html.

3. Quoted in *Twelve American Women,* p. 136.

References

Anticaglia, Elizabeth. *Twelve American Women.* Chicago: Nelson-Hall, 1975.

"Biographical Sketch of Jane Addams." On the web site of Jane Addams Hull-House Museum, University of Illinois at Chicago, www.uic.edu/jaddams/hull/ja_bio.html.

Diliberto, Gioia. *A Useful Woman: The Early Life of Jane Addams.* New York: Lisa Drew/Scribner, 1999.

"Jane Addams—Biography." On the web site of

Nobelprize.org, nobelprize.org/peace/laureates/1931/addams-bio.html.

Luft, Margaret. "Jane Adams: Hull House." On the web site of Hull House, www.hullhouse.org/about.asp.

Tims, Margaret. *Jane Addams of Hull House: 1860–1935.* New York: Macmillan, 1961.

Jim Thorpe

Notes

1. Abel Kiviat, quoted in *Contemporary Heroes and Heroines,* book 2, p. 482.

2. Oren Lyons, quoted in *Idols of the Game,* p. 75.

References

Garraty, John A., and Mark C. Carnes, gen. ed. *American National Biography.* New York: Oxford University Press, 1999.

Lipsyte, Robert, and Peter Levine. *Idols of the Game: A Sporting History of the American Century.* Atlanta: Turner Publishing, 1995.

Straub, Deborah Gillan, ed. *Contemporary Heroes and Heroines,* book 2. Detroit: Gale Research, 1992.

Sullivan, George. *Sports Great Lives.* New York: Charles Scribner's Sons, 1988.

Amelia Earhart

Notes

1. Amelia Earhart, quoted in "America's Story," on the web site of the Library of Congress, www.americaslibrary.gov/cgi-bin/page.cgi/aa/explorers/earhart/learns_1.

2. Amelia Earhart, letter to her husband, George Putnam, quoted on the Official Amelia Earhart web site, www.ameliaearhart.com/about/biography.html.

References

"Amelia Earhart: Celebrating One Hundred Years of Flight." On the Official Amelia Earhart web site, www.ameliaearhart.com/home.php.

"Amelia Earhart." On the web site of the Library of Congress, www.americaslibrary.gov/cgi-bin/page.cgi/aa/explorers/earhart.

"Amelia Earhart." On the web site of the Amelia Earhart Birthplace Museum, www.ameliaearhartmuseum.org/index.html

Goldstein, Donald M., and Katherine V. Dillon. *Amelia: The Centennial Biography of an Aviation Pioneer.* Washington: Brassey's, 1997.

Lovell, Mary S. *The Sound of Wings: The Life of Amelia Earhart.* New York: St. Martin's Press, 1989.

Rich, Doris L. *Amelia Earhart: A Biography.* Washington: Smithsonian Institution, 1989.

Franz Boas

Notes

1. Ruth Benedict, quoted in "What Is Anthropology," on the web site of Radford University, www.radford.edu/~soc-anth/whatanth.html.

References

"Biographical Focus: Franz Boas (1858–1942)," in "Introduction to Social Sciences." On the web site of Lewis-Clark State College, www.lcsc.edu/ss150/u3s2p1.htm.

"Franz Boas." On the web site of Anthropology Biography Web of Minnesota State University, www.mnsu.edu/emuseum/information/biography/abcde/boas_franz.html.

"Franz Boas." On the web site of Columbia University, c250.columbia.edu/c250_celebrates/remarkable_columbians/franz_boas.html.

Kroeber, A.L., et al. "Franz Boas." In *American Anthropologist,* New Series. Vol. 45, no. 3, pt. 2, July–September 1943. Reprinted in *Memoirs* by the American Anthropological Association. New York: Kraus Reprint, 1969.

"The Professor: Franz Boas." On the web site of the American Studies program at the University of Virginia, xroads.virginia.edu/~MA01/Grand-Jean/Hurston/Chapters/professor.html.

Rohner, Ronald P. "Franz Boas: Ethnographer on the Northwest." In *Pioneers of American Anthropology: The Uses of Biography,* edited by June Helm. Seattle, Washington: University of Washington Press, 1966.

Louis Armstrong

Notes

1. Louis Armstrong, introduction to *It's a Wonderful World,* 1970, quoted in "Louis Armstrong: A Cultural Legacy."

2. Louis Armstrong, quoted in "Louis 'Satchmo' Armstrong: The Greatest Musician in History," on the web site of Duke University, www.music.duke.edu/jazz_archive/artists/armstrong.louis/29/.

References

Crouch, Stanley. "Louis Armstrong," *The Time 100.* Text online at www.time.com/time/time100/artists/profile/armstrong.html.

Garraty, John A., and Mark C. Carnes, gen. ed. "Louis Armstrong," in *American National Biography*. New York: Oxford University Press, 1999.

"Louis Armstrong: A Cultural Legacy." On the web site of the Smithsonian National Portrait Gallery, www.npg.si.edu/exh/armstrong/.

"Louis Armstrong Biography." On the web site of the Louis Armstrong House and Archives, www.satchmo.net/bio/.

Travis, Dempsey J. *The Louis Armstrong Odyssey: From Jane Alley to America's Jazz Ambassador*. Chicago: Urban Research Press, 1997.

John Glenn

Notes

1. John Glenn, quoted in Tamara Lytle, "Glenn, Nelson Faced Flight Risks," *Orlando Sentinel*, February 2, 2003. Text online at www.orlandosentinel.com/news/custom/space/orl-asecssnelson02020203feb02,0,1054430.story.

2. John Glenn, quoted in *Famous in America: The Passion to Succeed*, p. 83.

3. John Glenn, *John Glenn: A Memoir*, p. 276. Glenn wrote these words soon after landing from his flight in the Mercury capsule. He filled out a form from NASA. It asked, "What would you like to say first?"

References

"Biographical Data" on John Glenn, on the web site of NASA, www.jsc.nasa.gov/Bios/htmlbios/glenn-j.html.

Carroll, Peter N. *Famous in America: The Passion to Succeed*. New York: E.P. Dutton, 1985.

Glenn, John, with Nick Taylor. *John Glenn: A Memoir*. New York: Bantam Books, 1999.

"A History of Manned Space Missions." On the web site Windows to the Universe, www.windows.ucar.edu/tour/link=/space_missions/manned_table.html.

Web site of the National Aeronautics and Space Administration History Office, www.hq.nasa.gov/office/pao/History/.

Amy Tan

Notes

1. Amy Tan, "Thinly Disguised Memoir," in *The Opposite of Fate: A Book of Musings*, p. 112.

2. Amy Tan, quoted in *Contemporary Authors: New Revision Series*, p. 419.

3. Amy Tan, "The Best Stories," in *The Opposite of Fate: A Book of Musings*, p. 354.

References

"Amy Tan." On the web site of the Academy of Achievement, www.achievement.org/autodoc/page/tan0pro-1.

Giles, James R., and Wanda H. Giles, ed. *American Novelists Since World War II*, 5th series, *Dictionary of Literary Biography*, Vol. 173. Detroit: Gale Research, 1996.

Hayes, Dwayne D., and Joyce Nakamura, man. ed. *Contemporary Authors: New Revision Series*, Vol. 105. Farmington Hills, MI: Gale Group, 2002.

Tan, Amy. *The Opposite of Fate: A Book of Musings*. New York: G.P. Putnam's Sons, 2003.

Web site of the Rock Bottom Remainders, www.rockbottomremainders.com.

Jaime Escalante

Notes

1. Jaime Escalante, quoted in "Excellence: Do It Right the First Time."

2. Ann Plato, quoted in Bert James Loewenberg and Ruth Bogin, *Black Women in Nineteenth-Century American Life*, part 2, University Park, PA: Pennsylvania State University Press, 1976.

References

Byers, Ann. *Jaime Escalante: Sensational Teacher*. Springfield, NJ: Enslow Publishers, 1996.

Hanson, Wayne, and Bob Graves. "Excellence: Do It Right the First Time: An Interview with Jaime Escalante," in "Visionaries: Creators of Worlds," *Government Technology: Visions*, Feb. 1998. Text online at www.govtech.net/magazine/visions/feb98vision/escalante.php.

"Jaime Escalante." On the web site of the National Teachers Hall of Fame, www.nthf.org/escalante.htm.

Mathews, Jay. *Escalante: The Best Teacher in America*. New York: Henry Holt, 1988.

Santana, Alfredo. "Jaime Escalante" in "PCC Spotlight." On the web site of Pasadena City College, www.pasadena.edu/about/history/alumni/escalante/escalante.cfm.

"The Jaime Escalante Math Program." On the web site of *The Futures Channel*, www.thefutureschannel.com/escalante_math_program.htm.